1001 Natural Logical Consequences

Specific Solutions to Help Kids Behave

By
Madalyn Skiles

PublishAmerica
Baltimore

© 2006 by Madalyn Skiles.
All rights reserved. No part of this book may be reproduced, stored in a retrieval system or transmitted in any form or by any means without the prior written permission of the publishers, except by a reviewer who may quote brief passages in a review to be printed in a newspaper, magazine or journal.

First printing

At the specific preference of the author, PublishAmerica allowed this work to remain exactly as the author intended, verbatim, without editorial input.

ISBN: 1-4241-5696-3
PUBLISHED BY PUBLISHAMERICA, LLLP
www.publishamerica.com
Baltimore

Printed in the United States of America

I would like to dedicate this book to Rosalie Gatson who was a living example of the fact that although no parent is perfect, all parents can be adequate. It is a form of gratitude for the years of dedicated work she gave to the Therapeutic Foster Care Program and her undying faith in me. I would echo her hope that it would result in less children being hurt, and more parents feeling happy. I trust she is now in the land she dreamed of—where kids no longer hurt. And to my mother: whose stable faith in me often kept me going.

I must also remember Debbie Smith, Teri White and the many other therapists who have helped me through the years. Last but surely not least to every child who has given me the opportunity to parent them. Surely if a book was to be written they were the practice group. Thanks munchkins.

Madalyn Skiles

Contents

Introduction 9
Why's and Why Me's 11
An Ounce of Prevention 13
Building a Carefree Home 16

Anger, the Red Demon

Angry Behaviors and Logical Consequences 22
Hollering at Someone 22
Foot Stomping 24
Door Slamming 26
Arguing 28
Refusing to Follow Instructions 29
Breaking Things 30
Hitting You 33
Hitting Self 34
Biting 36
Spitting 38
Fire Starting 40
Temper Tantrums 42
Throwing Things 44
Cursing 46
Hurting Animals 48

Sadness, the Invisible Prison

Locks Self in Room 52
Won't Talk 54
Doesn't Do Chores 56
Won't Involve Self 58
Poor School Grades 60
Won't Give Affection 62
Suicide Threats 64
Has No Friends 66

Doesn't Listen	68
Hurting Self	70
Whining	72

Sexual Behavior, the Shocking Mask

Sneaking Out	76
Wrong Friends	78
Dresses Inappropriate	80
Making Advances	82
Caught Having Sex	84
Public Masturbation	86
Sexual Language	88
Exposing Self	90
Playing with Feces	92
Wrong Care of Sanitary Napkins	94
Touching or Hugging Sexually	96
Has Pornographic Literature	98
Making Sexual Gestures	100
Fear of Opposite Sex	102

The Little Princess, Careless Behavior

Doesn't Pick Up	106
Steals Property	108
Won't Return Things	110
Loses Things	112
Dresses Poorly	114
Incomplete Chores	116
Incomplete Schoolwork	118
Daydreaming	120
Wastes Food	122
Doesn't Keep You Informed	124
Bed Wetting	126
Skipping School	128
Overuses Products	130
Doesn't Clean Room	132

Set up Behaviors

Loud Music 136
Interrupting 138
Constant Chattering 140
Shows Off 142
Blames Others 144
Minimizing 146
Belittles 148
Hiding Things 150
Tattles 152
Talks down about You to Others 154
Fakes Sickness 156
Gets in the Way of Others 158
Pouting 160
Spends Too Much Time at Friends 162
Making Faces 164
Finicky Eater 166

Fearful Behavior

Lying 170
Making Impulsive Decisions 172
Stealing Food 174
Clinging to You 176
Won't Go to School 178
Chronic Complaining 180
Agrees with Everyone 182
Won't Make Decisions 184
Has Anxiety Attacks 186
Won't Go to Bed 188
Has Nightmares 190
Can't Sleep 192
Making up Wild Stories 194

Vehicle Misuse, the Daily Roller Coaster
Taking Car Without Permission 198
Refusing to Stay in the Seat Belt 200
Distracting Behavior in Car 202
Opens Car Door When Moving 204
Dangerous Bike Riding 206
Doesn't Obey Traffic Laws 208
Grabs Things in the Car 210
Letting Other People Use Vehicle 212
Hanging out the Window 214
Hollers out the Window 216

Addictive Behavior, the Mysterious Maze
Compulsive Cleaning or Movement 220
Drinking Alcohol 222
Smoking Cigarettes 224
Using Drugs 226
Compulsive Eating 228

Bigotry, Born Better People
Name Calling 232
Joining Questionable Groups 234

Catch Them Being Good 236

Introduction

I start this book with somewhat of a tongue in cheek attitude, realizing of all the professions that do not fit into manuals, parenting probably comes highest on the list. To work a lifetime for no pay, to be expected to know all things, to be on constant call and seldom appreciated, to always be wrong in some area, and to accept all this gladly, that is the job description of a parent. If we are to believe all past cultures and most religions however, it is the most rewarding job we can have. It is the heritage each of us may leave the earth. It is a little piece of ourselves that will live forever. But, what are we to do as society changes and guidelines change? I have chosen to change with them knowing only that kids still need to be raised, and for that they need parents.

I suppose, in order to let you know who I am, I will share that I have been a mom for thirty years. I was first a mom to my own children, then a step-mom, next a mom to the children of friends who were at their wits' end. From there I became a foster mom, and finally a therapeutic foster mom; parenting solely those kids who had behavioral and emotional problems. I also teach MAPPS, a training and preparation program for parents who wish to foster children.

I started out as an inadequate mom at fifteen years of age and through the years of trying to do it "my way" I realized things were not getting better. I was going to need some help if I was to raise my children rather than slay them. I began to search for answers. And I found them. The infuriating part of parenting is, even as you grasp the answers, they change, or you change, and what worked once, no longer works, ad infinitum.

As you can probably guess by now I am not writing a know it all, fix it all book. What I am hoping for is a series of guidelines that will help you come up with some quick consequences for some of the crazy behaviors that your children are bound to display. Since the majority of my experience has been with teenagers you may find that many of these answers are not age appropriate. Don't be afraid to scale them down or up. Discard them if they are ineffective, and by all means add to the list. The truth is that you can not have too many choices when it comes to having quick answers for your kid's behaviors. The only real guarantee I will make is that no matter how many answers you have, the day will come when you wish you had more.

So without any further ado let us take a look at kids and their behaviors and the behaviors we want from them.

Why's and Why Me's

Why do my kids act the way they do, and why do they act even more that way with me? That is the number one question I think most parents ask themselves and other specialists. Please understand that your little human being is not setting out in the morning to deliberately ruin your day. They, like us adults, have needs and make choices to get those needs met. They, like us, don't particularly like rules. We all seem to be born with a built in denial system that says, "It can't happen to me." We all need boundaries and all of us, at times, resent them. The simple truth is that children misbehave because they are human and they particularly misbehave with you because they feel pretty safe in knowing what you will and won't do to them. They are comfortable with you and for the most part, we can thank God for that.

That is the nature of the beast, but how do we set the boundaries *we* need and still help our kids feel content and safe at the same time? The old system of spank them all soundly and put them to bed is not a good answer anymore for a number of reasons. One of the best is that there is a chance you could hit them too hard or have your actions misinterpreted and risk losing one of the most priceless possessions you have. The second is, that in a society using less and less corporal discipline at any level, you will be perceived by your children as the unfair parent and by being that, they have a built in reason to not trust anything you say. Along the lines of an experienced parent, on a scale of one to ten, I rate this at about a *two* in effectiveness. I had to accept the fact that although it was quick and easy as a form of discipline, it simply did not get the long term **results** which I wanted.

"Spare the rod and spoil the child" is one of the most misunderstood verses that I know of. A rod was an instrument used for guiding sheep. It provided a boundary which kept them heading in the right direction. Never would the sheepherder beat his sheep; it was neither necessary nor helpful. In this context, I agree wholly with the verse. If I don't direct my children and provide boundaries, I will truly spoil, or the words I prefer are, ruin them. That left me in the dilemma of what to do instead. I found that **natural and logical consequences** were without a doubt the easiest and most effective method that I could use for obtaining the desired behavior. That is, *when I could think of one.* I envisioned this book. If I wrote a simple manual, which a parent could glance at and find some answers, perhaps we would all be better off.

An Ounce of Prevention

This little piece of advice given long ago is still some of the best around. Do you want loving, cooperative, responsible children? Then by all means build it in. Find every opportunity to **catch them being good and let them know it**.

Studies have proven it takes *four* positive statements to prepare the mind to hear *one* negative statement. Listen to yourself as you talk to your children. What is it you are focusing on, where they are right or where they are wrong? To give someone a direction really means telling them where you want them to go and helping them get there. I have often heard a mother cry about an uncaring child only to see her in the next breath scolding him for hanging on her or saying to her child, "not now, I'm busy." If you are doing this you are really teaching your child that to care, means rejection. Although your words state your desire for affection, your actions say the opposite. How often would you want to hug your spouse if he or she responded with "Not now, can't you see I'm busy?" Children are simply little people. You will probably read this a lot throughout this manual. When I truly discovered it, I was on the road to being an effective parent.

"Do I build in responsibility," is another question well worth asking ourselves.

If I say things to myself like, it is too much trouble to get them to do it so I'll just do it myself; I am creating an irresponsible person. We often forget how long and hard won our own victories were, in our learning to do any task responsibly. I have found it much easier to look and see how close my child is to accomplishing the task and keep him trying, rather than to focus on how much of it he hasn't yet finished. To trust and expect our children to be a help to us, is probably a harder goal than to actually get them to do it.

Family meetings also make a good sounding off place, where you can give your children a chance to have a voice and still have some input into their choices. Everything in my home goes to a family vote. There have often been more children voting than adults. These kids have severe emotional problems. Yet, not once have I had a really bad judgment call come out of a family meeting. A word of caution here: as a primary care giver and moneymaker, although all choices are up to the family, I have all rights over my own belongings, just as they do over theirs. Therefore, a trip to Disney World is not out of the question…if…they are willing to hold car washes and sell lemonade to help raise the needed funds.

Do my children have a say in their own lives? I have found the absolute best way to **get** any child to do anything is to have them **want** to do it. For example, I have NEVER had a kid say, "Oh, gosh, I've got to get up—today is Christmas." We all respond positively to doing that which gives us pleasure.

Perhaps if we can build more commitment into our kids we will get more willingness out of them. I always try to let my children have a say in their lives. Many of the things we want our kids to do are really none of our business and would be far better left to them to decide.

I really don't have to tell them what cereal to eat, what clothes to wear, how to comb their hair, and in what order their toys need to be arranged, to name a few choices that I was determined to make for my children at one point. Are my directions clear? Too often I will expect my children to know what I want. I am then upset when they don't. One of the most revealing adventures I ever had was learning how to make a chart. Many of the things that upset me were really not being understood or followed through on because of lack of reward and no complete understanding of what I wanted.

I use a chart with older children by saying it is a schedule and reward home management sheet. This eliminates the perceived *childishness* of a chart system by the children. Don't forget rewards are not necessarily monetary. A car ride to a friend or a chore you do for them are good examples of rewards that cost nothing. In my house we all are responsible for our own clothes. It is amazing what one can get in lieu of pants being hemmed.

I personally like charts that are large and can be posted in an obvious place. A simple guideline would be to list the day, the responsibility, and who is accountable, next leave a place to mark when it was done. I made a prize box. It was a small box and in it I wrote a number of extras that they could gain. Such as a free ride to town, an extra snack, homemade cookies, choice of meal. When they had accomplished 10 responsibilities they got to go in the box and see which one they picked. I have also used charts where A gets you B. A equaling cleaning your room, gets you B free time. Both work, I simply found that everyone enjoys the surprise factor of the box; kind of like a home version of the lotto.

In summary of this section I will list some simple questions I ask myself to make sure I am on the right track, because there is always the chance the kids are already following and I am simply leading them the wrong way.

1. How many of my sentences today have been praise rather than criticism? If my ratio is not 4 to 1, I correct it *promptly*.
2. Is the action I am asking one which I practice myself? If it is not, perhaps I better form a team with my child and work on it together.
3. Is what I am asking of my child really building in the behavior I want?
4. Have I asked for my child's feelings about my request?
5. Is this really any of my business?
6. What can I do to creatively solve this problem? Is that my goal, or do I wish to win or punish?
7. Have I been clear in what I want and allowed for a child's lessened skills?

As we begin to ask ourselves these questions we begin to see that the problem is as much us as it is them. This is of use only in making us a bit more tolerant of their failings.

Building a Carefree Home

I think I speak for most of us when I say we would like our home to run like Ozzie and Harriet's home on TV. Only that is television. However, there are ways to build in a home life that is peaceful and certainly functional. It is also *nowhere near as hard as you might think*. Any home starts with a foundation. Let us look at the foundation of your home. Mom, how well do you know what is expected of you, and how realistic it is? Do you and Dad agree on how the house is run? Do you take time **together** and take time for yourself **apart**? Are you happy with each other? I can almost hear myself complaining and justifying when I was first asked these questions. Let me assure you, you do not need to be perfect nor have your life in complete order to be an *effective parent*. You do, however, need to know where it is not effective, so you can have a team effort to work on it. I have been a parent when I was happily married, unhappily married, single and dating. The only real difference I have discovered was whether or not I was **honest** in my appraisal of it. If I wasn't, then it affected my parenting. So ask yourselves those questions and use them as your foundation. If there is a weak area, ask for help or find someone who can give you some good suggestions on strengthening it.

Next, let us look at the building which rests on that foundation and what we want when we are done. Write this down, you will probably need your whole family to put in their thoughts. I will name some of the things that I find most of us want:

1. The right to our own time and space. A place that is *ours* and the right to spend some time how we want to spend it.
2. To feel safe at all times.
3. To be heard and to be included by other family members.

Not too many things to want, but almost everything is included in them. In order to achieve these things all family members are going to have to sacrifice a bit of themselves. List all the things that have to be done in your home. Next, divide it up so that everyone is carrying some of the chores. Hold in your mind that school and work both count as large chunks out of a person's day. Let everyone voice the part of the work they would prefer, then, get a list going. You are going to want to divide the available space. If you are like us, you are going to find that it breaks down into group space and individual space. Make sure everyone is able to have some space that is just theirs both to care for and to run to. One summer when I was overflowing with humans my Granddaughters came for the summer. In an effort to find some little spot that was solely hers we gave her the tree out front. I often looked at her perched in her tree and thought how it just might have saved our sanity that summer.

Now look at time. There needs to be time for each individual to be alone, time for the whole family to be together and time for a husband and wife to be alone together. If you are a single parent, you need time for male or female company. There needs to be time for work, and pleasure. Next, take a look at money. In most homes I find this is a harder subject to discuss honestly with our kids than sex.

Usually the adults in the home are the money makers and contributors, this does not need to be, but it is. Look at what you can afford and if there is not enough money to go around look for places to cut. Force your kids to do an honest appraisal of how much they cost you and if that could be subject to change. Are there ways they could meet some of their own needs for money? Perhaps some of their wants will need to be put on a shelf. No matter what your financial position allow your kids to know that they can be productive and meet some of their own needs. Even if they pick up some of the parents responsibilities and are paid for it. Basically, what we are responsible to give our children is three meals a day, a bed and safe housing, clothing, medical care, and everything after that is a want. Once they know their rights they begin to become aware of how many of their wants you are meeting.

This would be a good time to hold a **Family Meeting.**

There are a number of formats but I will share the one we use. We start with a moment of silence to clear our mind and get comfortable or to ask our God to join us. Although attendance is not mandatory it is strongly suggested. If you don't come to the family meeting you don't have a say and someone might just decide to go to a family outing on your prom night. All decisions are final but can be revoked in the next family meeting.

First, we address **issues**. This is any matter that affects the family; good or bad, such as upcoming appointments, managing washing machine times, family outings, anything that is a current or upcoming issue. Often this is the place to *vote* on *consequences* and let the kids have a vote too. They are much more willing to accept them when they have had a vote at the family meeting.

Next, we give verbal **hatchets**. This is anything we want to say to a person that is negative but really not subject to change. It might include something like "you really hurt my feelings at the store yesterday" or "you get a hatchet for interrupting me". This allows the family members to get things off their chests and avoid blowing up later by collecting these negative feelings.

Finally, we *always* finish with verbal **good strokes**. These are simply something about the other person that we like. We all love each other but don't often take the time to say what we love them for. This is a great time to do that.

During the family meeting we cannot comment or reply to either hatchets or good strokes. It is up to the individual to accept them or reject them as they see fit. We have found that by making sure we ***end on good strokes*** the meetings leave us feeling good about ourselves.

Having met and decided all this you are well on your way to having a functional house. Everything past this point comes under the heading of "how to keep it all going the way we planned it at the family meeting that bright day we set it on paper".

Try to have fun making it work; it truly is a fun adventure. Here are some tips to remember:
1. Appraise yourself
2. Appraise your relationships
3. Appraise your time
4. Appraise your money
5. **Hold *family meetings* at least 2 times a week**
6. Ask for help
7. Have a plan

Anger, the Red Demon

Of all the emotions that bring forth dread in the average parent I truly believe that anger gets top billing. Like it or lump it anger is a real feeling and not going to go away. The trick then is not so much to make our children not *be* angry as to teach them workable ways to **act** *when* they are angry.

First, let us take a look at the red demon so we can really know what we are combating. I like to think of emotions like a color chart I get at the paint store. I use red for anger because it seems to fit phrases like, "I saw red when that was done", or "I'm hot as fire about that". These seem to reinforce this color use. Now I may feel annoyed, vexed, or piqued at something. I think of those as shades of pink. If I am aggravated, angry, or mad I see those as a true red. If I hate, rage, or am furious I see them as a brick red or almost purple. In seeing them this way I can help myself and my kids take action and see how fast they need to take action on something. Brick needs immediate action, where pink can often be overlooked. You see, we humans all react to life differently and knowing what drives me and my children crazy helps us all to live in harmony. If harmony is the goal why give anger any time in our life?

The reason for that is simple, anger is a doing emotion. Many of the changes that get made are because someone got angry. It is a human's way of making our world a better place to live. To try to kill that emotion in our young would make a generation of sheep; people who would go along with anything just to keep the peace. For myself, when I am old and helpless, I hope there will be a generation of people who will get mad over injustices and fight to protect me if I need it. This is another of the basic truths we need to discover. Our children need to learn the things that are worth getting angry at. We need to realize that since they are learning, they will make mistakes, and many times get angry at a person rather than a principle. This is a place we can help, because we can give them the broader scope.

Picture this:

Johnny comes in screaming "I **hate** my sister. She is mean and I am going to hit her when she is sleeping tonight!" First response of any parent is, "No!! You will **NOT** hurt her." But let's look a little deeper and ask Johnny what happened. On the bus home sis decided to tell a cute story about Johnny wetting the bed and all of his friends were there. Do you see the picture change? Now if you are like me, the next thing you feel is a desire to publicly flog your daughter. You're where Johnny was when he walked in. However, I am going to broaden the scene even a little wider. You look at what principles Johnny believes in and how strongly.

He believes that people have a right to privacy about mistakes made at home and he has a deep sense of tact. These are some qualities you don't want to destroy in a person or he will be doing what his sister is doing a few years down the road. You point out these qualities to him and help him be more secure in his beliefs about himself. Chances are that by now the brick has turned to red if not to pink for Johnny. The problem will reappear, however, if some action is not taken. You will also have a great chance to teach Johnny some concrete things to do with his anger besides beating sis up while she sleeps.

Later on, I will give a number of choices on things you can suggest but for now I will use only one. You suggest that Johnny draw a picture of his sister and lock her and her big mouth up in the drawer for the present. Then you assure him that you will bring up the right to privacy at your **family meeting;** where you will be sure to mention how it might feel if sis's boyfriend realized that she was cruel to little children and told embarrassing stories in front of their friends. Johnny leaves feeling there is an answer to the problem. Sis will outgrow a disturbing behavior, and you feel a bit like Solomon, very wise and successful. Anger has served a good and useful purpose in your home this day.

Tips to remember:
1. Anger is real and will not go away
2. Anger serves a good purpose
3. Anger has shades and needs to be treated accordingly
4. You can teach your kids how to behave when angry
5. You can help them learn what makes them angry.
6. You can turn those reactions into principles.
7. You can see your own anger and handle it.

Angry Behaviors and Logical Consequences

Hollering at Someone

These are for children that are *willing* to cooperate in consequences.
1. Make them go back and rephrase it in the appropriate way.
2. Have them make a list of five ways they could have handled it better.
3. Young ones can *tell* you five ways.
4. Have them say four positive things about the person.
5. Have them whisper what they want to say for the next three to five minutes.
6. Have them write I will talk quietly five to ten times.
7. Have them go holler at the mirror what they said.
8. Have them apologize to the people they hollered at in front of the people who were present.
9. Have them state different times they were yelled at and how it made them feel.
10. Give them a 5 min time out until they are calm.

These are for children who are *unwilling* to cooperate in consequences.

11. Remove yourself and the person being hollered at from the room.
12. Give extra time and attention to the person being hollered at. Make it clear that this is necessary *because* they were hollered at. I like to use the time they were yelled at plus five minutes.
13. Have the person being yelled at refuse to respond to the yeller for at least half an hour but **NEVER** more than 2 hours.
14. Put television and radio on lowest setting in volume and let the person yelling know you are assuming their hearing is defective since they find it necessary to yell.
15. Have all other members whisper for a while again stating the reason to yeller.
16. Have all members tell yeller how it makes them feel and how they want to act when the person yells. This is best done at a family meeting when all are calm.
17. Have all members ignore the yeller until he can speak in a calm tone.

ADD METHODS YOU HAVE USED:

_____
_____
_____
_____

Foot Stomping

These are for children that are *willing* to cooperate in consequences.
18. Have them practice walking softly for five minutes
19. Have them repeat the phrase "Walk softly and carry a big stick." Explaining it was a Roosevelt motto.
20. Have them help repair a floor.
21. Put a fine box up and whenever feet are stomped put in a money amount toward its repair.
22. Have them draw a picture of their foot and what could be injured by stomping.
23. Make them go in socks for the rest of the evening to protect the floor.
24. Have them go outside and use welcome mat to vigorously wipe feet. Explain this is a healthy way to release that energy.
25. Have them give you five choices that could have used to release that angry energy.
26. Have them make a square of paper and allow them to stomp only within that.

1001 NATURAL LOGICAL CONSEQUENCES

These are for children that are *unwilling* to cooperate in consequences.

27. Remove all their shoes from their room (don't allow outside) only give them back the next day when they are headed out the door and with their assurance they will use the shoes properly.
28. Prepare a foot bath and allow no privileges until they have soaked their feet five minutes.
29. Buy out of child's allowance foot cushions assuring them they will need to get in the habit of buying them if they continue in that behavior.
30. Lock the door. When child comes home do not allow him in until they have given you their shoes. Remind them of the stomping. Allow them to earn the shoes back by walking softly.

ADD METHODS YOU HAVE USED:

_____
_____
_____
_____

Door Slamming

These are for children that are *willing* to cooperate in consequences.

31. Have them help repair a door. This will help them see the work involved should they break it.
32. Have them close the door softly about ten times.
33. Have the child write five to ten times "I will close the door quietly".
34. Have them shut the door softly then they can go slam a pillow on the bed.
35. Set up a fine jar for the logical consequence if the child continues to slam it they will break it and money will be needed to repair it.
36. Have the child state why a door is a good addition to a home and what its purpose is. An older child can do this in writing.

These are for children that are *unwilling* to cooperate in consequences.

37. Lock the door they are slamming thus forcing them to use the other door for the day.
38. Take their bedroom door off for the day explaining that they don't appreciate it. Allow them to earn it back with proper use of the other doors, or if you set a time limit I would advise you make it short.
39. Take an item of theirs in escrow to pay for the probable repairs of the door. Allow them to earn the item back by not slamming the door or one of the above consequences.
40. Build in a reward such as "Susan, you haven't slammed the door all day so I have saved enough time not reminding you that we can play a game of cards".

ADD METHODS YOU HAVE USED:
_____
_____
_____
_____

Arguing

These are for children that are *willing* to cooperate in consequences.
41. Suggest they bring it up at a **family meeting**.
42. Explain how the arguing makes you feel. Keep focus on arguing behavior NOT the issue.
43. Have them write their argument.
44. Have them tell their point of view to a third non involved party; friend, hotline, minister.
45. Have them join a debating class at school.

These are for children that are *unwilling* to cooperate in consequences.
46. Refuse to speak to them on that subject any longer.
47. Leave the room for five minutes when they start to argue.
48. Refuse to speak or make eye contact for the next three to five minutes.
49. Turn on T.V. or radio and direct their attention there.

ADD METHODS YOU HAVE USED:

_____
_____
_____
_____

Refusing to Follow Instructions
(Obviously unwilling)

50. Stop all activities until the child has done what you have requested. Assure them that as soon as they do what you ask, things will go back to normal.
51. Simply stop and look at the child. Make no forward move nor continue to discuss the matter. As soon as the child makes some move, simply state you are waiting for them to follow your instruction. Assure them that you will be glad to get on with life as soon as they follow your instruction.
52. State that it is the child's choice, but if you cannot get your request from them, then the next time they make a request they can expect you will not follow it. Do nothing until their next request, then simply say "no", reminding the child of their previous choice).
53. Follow through the behavior for the child. In other words, if the child says no, I won't pick up my toys, you can say: "Well what do you think will happen if you choose that, what will I do?" Continue until you are sure the child can see the consequences of refusing or saying "no".
54. Ignore the behavior, then, at a later time, bring it up at the **family meeting**. (See introduction) At that time address the unwillingness and the consequence for that. Make sure it is something that the child doesn't have to participate in, for instance, no one listen to their request for the next two hours.
55. Say nothing but make a chart. Place it in a conspicuous place and draw a big sad face for every time the child says no. Three noes loses a request of theirs.

ADD METHODS YOU HAVE USED:

_____

_____

_____

Breaking Things

These are for children that are *willing* to cooperate in consequences.

56. Have them repair the item they have broken
57. Have them do work to an equivalent of the cost of the item.
58. Have them hold a yard sale to pay off the equivalent cost of the item.
59. Have them do a report on vandalism.

These are for children that are *unwilling* to cooperate in consequences.
60. Take the privilege of using similar items away for a time period. One day to one week.
61. Confiscate item of similar value and bring child with you while you sell it to a consignment shop.
62. Confiscate item of greater value and allow him to 'buy' it back by paying you the amount of the item.
63. Have a policeman come and talk to him on the legal consequences of vandalism.
64. *Withhold gas money you would have spent on child taking them places, toward broken item.
65. *Withhold snack money and keep toward the cost of the item.

*Note: on the above I strongly advise you allow the child at any time to choose to pay for the item himself. The reason for this is that if a child gets to the point of cooperation in consequences everyone's life becomes much easier.

ADD METHODS YOU HAVE USED:

_____
_____

Hitting Others

These are for children that are *willing* to cooperate in consequences.
66. Have child spend half an hour caring for person they have hit.
67. Have child write a letter of apology (more than just I am sorry).
68. Have them spread there arms and do not allow them within that distance of the other person for half an hour to a day.
69. Have them sit apposing each other and resolve their problem by negotiating
70. Send child to a quiet place and allow their return only when they can state other options they could have used.
71. Have them keep an object in their hands ball of yarn works well, to remind them not to hit. Agree they will pick that up whenever they feel themselves getting angry.
72. Have them go to Bible or spiritual book and seek, then tell you a spiritual answer.

These are for children that are *unwilling* to cooperate in consequences.
73. Hold an emergency **family meeting** and have the group come up with alternatives.
74. Take the party that is hit and spend quality time with them explaining to hitter that now the other person needs this attention. *
75. Have the entire family confront the issue at the next **family meeting** and avoid being geographically close to the hitter.
76. Take an item of worth from hitter and give it to the person hit as monetary restitution. Allow hitter the right to earn it back with acts of kindness or as the victim chooses work.*
77. Little children may be restrained and held in a chair for no longer than two to five minutes. Stress you will let go as soon as they show they will sit there by themselves.**

* **BE CAREFUL** with this as often it may reward a child that sets another child up to hit. I have found it very effective with children that just lash out at the closest person.

** To safely restrain a youngster it is *imperative* that you receive training on correct procedures. We **strongly suggest** that you **NEVER RESTRAIN A CHILD UNTIL YOU RECEIVE EXPERT TRAINING.**

There are many programs such as ACT Training (Aggression Control Techniques) and NCI Training (Nonviolent Crisis Intervention). In this way you can be sure you will not injure a child. Contact your local mental health organization about such classes. They are usually inexpensive and only last a day or two.

ADD METHODS YOU HAVE USED:

_____
_____
_____
_____

Hitting You

These are for children that are *willing* to cooperate in consequences.

78. Do not allow child in car unless seated in position furthest from you. Explain that you feel unsafe close to child and that must be earned back by showing different behaviors when angry.
79. Make a contract that all hot issues are to be prayed about together before they are discussed.
80. Have all angry remarks written to you.
81. Have them spend a nurturing time, making up to you for hurting you.
82. Allow them to go nowhere without you since you cannot be sure they will not hurt someone.

These are for children that are *unwilling* to cooperate in consequences.

83. Withdraw all car privileges until child earns back a feeling of trust by showing other behaviors when angry.
84. Refuse to discuss any angry topics except at **family meetings**.
85. Call the police and file charges—for younger ones have the police talk to them.
86. Refuse to be in the same room with them for one or two days unless someone else is present.
87. Give yourself a special treat in front of them explaining you must now nurture yourself because you were hurt by them.

ADD METHODS YOU HAVE USED:

_____
_____
_____
_____

Hitting Self

I have put this behavior down twice because in essence there are two different behaviors that respond to very different consequences. This is the child who is angry and hits or hurts himself to get even with you.

These are for children that are *willing* to cooperate in consequences.
88. Tell child to hit the bed instead of themselves.
89. At a family meeting share alternatives to hitting self. Some might include running, digging hole, banging wood.
90. Have them spend two to five minutes pounding on couch or bed.
91. Have them take a *RED* crayon and color hard for a few minutes. You can even have an angry crayon set aside.
92. Tell them to blow up and pop five balloons then they can continue if they want.

These are for children that are *unwilling* to cooperate in consequences.

93. Walk away and assure child you will come back if they stop
94. In a firm tone of voice, tell child that kind of behavior will force you to take privileges starting with their right to be alone.*
95. You can restrain a child but use caution check footnote on behavior (**7**) about proper training.*
96. Place yourself within eye contact but out of hitting range and quietly watch stating: *"we will talk when you stop hurting yourself"*.
97. After the fact, you can remove all clothes but long sleeves and slacks saying you want child to have as much protection from themselves as possible. Allow them to earn the clothes back by handling anger in a different manner.

**BE CAREFUL—MAKE SURE CHILD IS NOT HURT—GET MEDICAL ATTENTION IMMEDIATELY IF THE CHILD IS HURT. THIS MAY BACKFIRE AND CREATE MORE INTENSIFIED BEHAVIOR. IF THAT HAPPENS STOP AND USE A DIFFERENT CONSEQUENCE, SEEK PROFESSIONAL HELP!

ADD METHODS YOU HAVE USED:

_____
_____
_____
_____

Biting

These are for children that are *willing* to cooperate in consequences.

98. I find that having child spend time nurturing the victim is a good teaching consequence.
99. Have child practice biting their tongue (*not hard enough to damage themselves*) but a couple of days having two minutes practice a day can be a great reminder.
100. Have the child take 5 min time out until they can give you five ways they could have acted instead.
101. Allow the victim to choose a non violent consequence for the child.
102. Have a fine to cover cost of band-aids and antiseptic that will have to be used.
103. Explore the reason for biting and build in a reward for any time biter takes a non violent solution. Kids may manipulate this somewhat for the reward but because I find the behavior dangerous I don't mind.

These are for children that are *unwilling* to cooperate in consequences.

104. Remove the person who was bitten from room and later build in quality time with the victim.
105. Withhold all communication from the biter for a period of ten minutes to an hour explaining you are extremely displeased at this behavior.
106. Withdraw communication but only until biter is willing to participate in one of the above consequences.
107. You can use restraint to stop this initially but I would advise caution or the person being bit could be injured worse. *(See problem 7 above for instruction on where to get training.)**
108. Wait until a **family meeting** and use the group to take some privilege such as not being in car or watching TV with the victim for a few days. This will take either car rides or TV away from the offender yet still match the crime since there is a danger of them being together.

ADD METHODS YOU HAVE USED:

_____
_____
_____
_____

Spitting

These are for children that are *willing* to cooperate in consequences.
109. Have the child clean it up.
110. Have child carry a small can in the house to spit in for the rest of the day.
111. Have child take time to come up with four other behaviors they could have used and spend three to five minutes practicing one of them
112. If child spit at someone have them write an apology note and or buy them a card.
113. Give them a cleaning assignment like the bathroom sink so they can be proficient in cleaning after bodily fluid since they choose to misuse them.

These are for children that are *unwilling* to cooperate in consequences.

114. You clean it up and *DO NOT SAY A WORD*. When child tries to talk to you explain that you are waiting for an apology for making you clean up their mess.
115. Next few times you go out or go to engage in the behavior where the spitting occurred ask child if they are planning on spitting because you won't take them if they are.
116. Have the family confront the behavior and give their general feelings on it.
117. Take away gum and candy for a week explaining you are not sure you can trust what they will do with the extra saliva since they're not handling what they have now appropriately.
118. For the next few days whenever child comes in ask if they are planning on spitting explaining you just want to know so you can keep a napkin handy. This friendly re-enforcer can be a powerful tool in breaking unacceptable behaviors.

ADD METHODS YOU HAVE USED:

_____
_____
_____
_____

Fire Starting

I need to say that this is an extremely *dangerous behavior* and can be *life threatening* to a number of people. If a child has been involved in this more than once, you will need to get them to a **therapist** who is trained to handle very angry children.

These are for children that are *willing* to cooperate in consequences.

119. Make all areas where fire is used (kitchen, living room if there is a fireplace, cook-out areas) off limits until you see signs of less anger and more control.
120. Have them participate in a fire safety program. Ask for a report verbal or written to be brought to the family meeting.
121. Have them hold fire drills for the next couple of weeks at the house.
122. Take all alone privileges away until they can earn back the trust by showing appropriate ways to express anger.
123. Have them do a fire awareness skit for the family and have them find pictures of either burn victims or property.
124. Have them write ten times each day for a week "Matches are dangerous I will give them to an adult".

These are for children that are *unwilling* to participate in consequences.

125. Have a daily room search for the next week or two to make sure there are no lighters or matches in room.
126. Turn off all fire starting equipment nightly and do a house check to make sure all lighters etc. are not within reach.
127. Take away the right to go to all cook-outs or such for a month. Explaining that child can not be trusted because of the behavior.
128. Go to peers and school with child and make them aware of the problem.

ADD METHODS YOU HAVE USED:

_____
_____
_____
_____

Temper Tantrums

These are for children that are *willing* to cooperate in consequences.

129. At the **family meeting** have child put a time limit on the temper tantrum. Ask how long they will have the next one. Come up with a plan to shorten the time after each one. Remind child at the start of the tantrum and right before time is up.
130. Limit the place child can hold a tantrum. I like beds, they cannot hurt themselves if they bang, but their room or the couch, outside, are all choices.
131. Allow the tantrum only after a two minute hug. This will backfire if you are angry and cannot hug the child while this is going on.
132. Set a goal for a week or a day depending on frequency and offer a small reward for behavior not occurring; extra TV time or to bed fifteen minutes later. Be sure to connect it with the behavior. "I enjoyed you so much because there were no tantrums how would you like to stay up another fifteen minutes tonight".
133. Limit behavior to parts. Today you may scream but we are not going to kick. Change these as time goes on. Then form a plan to move on to more appropriate ways to handle anger.

These are for children that are *unwilling* to cooperate in consequences.

134. Totally ignore the behavior. Make a positive comment when it is over such as boy is it good to have you back to yourself.
135. At a **family meeting** have group share the impact of behavior on them and if any have ever done it how and why they chose to stop.
136. If they bang themselves carefully place a soft object under them and let them know they are responsible to put it away when they are done.
137. Stop what you are doing and scream. Not at them but just scream using shock value sometimes will help them see themselves as others see them. Stop as soon as they do and make some comment on how it felt to you to scream.
138. Keeping your voice tone gentle express a willingness to discuss the problem if and when they stop.

ADD METHODS YOU HAVE USED:
_____
_____
_____
_____

Throwing Things

Throwing things in not really the problem. I have often used this as a healthy vent for anger. The problem is where and what is being thrown, so I focus on that in my consequences.

These are for children that are *willing* to cooperate in consequences.//
139. Agree to throw a basketball in the hoop when angry.
140. Get a Nerf ball and agree it can be thrown at an empty wall in child's bedroom.
141. Plan to play a game of catch when the child wants to throw something. Use a beach ball for this as I have found they will throw pretty hard when angry.
142. Use balloons and let them throw as hard and anywhere they want.
143. Allow them to have a golf ball and to throw it on the cement sidewalk as hard as they want.

These are for children that are *unwilling* to cooperate in consequences.

144. Take the object away until the child can show they have control enough to have it.
145. Force restitution for item by either taking an item of equal value or allowing child the choice to pay for the item.
146. Immediately remove all hard items from child's room stressing that the throwing of things presents a danger.
147. For the next day do not give child anything before first asking if they are going to throw it.
148. Write a list of ten reasons why it is not wise to throw things and post it in child's room.
149. Post a list of items that can be safely thrown in child's room.
150. Bring the issue up at a **family meeting** and let group come up with what is o.k. and not o.k. to throw.

ADD METHODS YOU HAVE USED:

_____
_____
_____
_____

Cursing

These are for children that are *willing* to cooperate in consequences.
151. Have child say five words they could have used instead.
152. Have a fine for anyone who uses foul language. This must go for everyone in the house.
153. Have child tell you places where that behavior would be acceptable. Then get an agreement to go to one of those places whenever they want to curse.
154. Have the child go in bedroom and repeat what he said into an open drawer. Close the drawer and tell them those words are now locked in there and in order to curse they must first go get them out.
155. Choose an alternate word: sugar for sh*t and have them use it at least seven times in the conversation the next day.

These are for children that are *unwilling* to cooperate in consequences.

156. Ignore the behavior and make sure you do not use foul language reinforcing why you choose not to curse
157. If behavior is used by a friend, when friend comes to visit do not allow them in unless they assure you there will be no foul language.
158. Withdraw all movies that have foul language until child can show that they do not affect his or her language. I would advise this is very short term as in a day and no longer than a week.
159. Repeat words back to child using alternate words and state that you expect to hear those words before some privilege occurs; as in before your bedtime story, or you use the phone, or snack. Do not give the reward until child says word. The trick to this is not to bring it up again.
160. Walk away when the language is used. Refuse to converse with child until you receive an apology. I find firm works much better than angry, in voice tone and attitude. I simply state I am a person who is offended by that and I expect anyone who uses it to apologize.

ADD METHODS YOU HAVE USED:

_____
_____
_____
_____

Hurting Animals

This is a behavior that has two definite patterns. One is the child who simply has not learned proper care of animals and the other a child who is taking out their anger on animals. Knowing which one is your child's goal will help you choose the consequence that is most effective.

These are for children that are *willing* to cooperate in consequences.
161. Have child spend a monitored teaching time with animal where you can reinforce proper touching.
162. Have child get a book from the library on care of animals and don't allow them near animal until they can give you facts they have learned.
163. Put a deposit on hold before they are allowed to touch animal. In other words "You need to give me something I can sell in case you hurt the dog. I will give it back when you are done playing with the dog if you have not hurt him."
164. Have them call S.P.C.A. and get information on the care of animals. I like to have them practice caring for animals after they get that skill.
165. Have them write or give you a report on the losses each family member would experience if animal was gone or on the joys of having a pet.
166. Have them pay for some of the costs that are involved, food or medicine. Let them know you feel they need to be more invested in a pet so they will understand your concern.

These are for children that are *unwilling* to cooperate in consequences.

167. Do not allow the animal in the room they are in. Use this for only short term, a few hours since it requires a lot of monitoring. Stress you are trusting them not to hurt the animal when you let them together again.
168. Call the S.P.C.A. and ask them to come and explain the process they use when someone has hurt an animal. Be very honest letting them know the child is hurting animals.
169. Offer a reward for each day child does not hurt the animal. Let the reward be connected with the animal, such as giving the dog a treat, or letting the bird sit on their finger.
170. Let the animal go. This is a harsh choice but if the behavior continues it is the kindest for the animal and teaches the child there is a responsibility level that if you don't meet you will lose a pet. I would do this by a family vote unless the animal is solely the child's.

ADD METHODS YOU HAVE USED:

_____
_____
_____
_____

Sadness, the Invisible Prison

I call sad the invisible prison because that is what it seems to be. Although you can't see the bars, the children are locked within themselves unable to get free to enjoy life and join in the world. The solution always seems to be in getting the key that will free them from their solitary thoughts and world.

I say again that parents must realize that all behaviors are a reaction to feelings and all feelings are there for a reason. Sadness I believe is there to help us slow down and heal from a hurt. Sadness, unlike anger does not usually threaten us. For this reason if for no other it is one of the feelings when expressed inappropriately is likely to have secondary gains. In other words I, as a parent, have often added to the problem by catering to the sad child and overlooking behaviors that were not at all acceptable, but were not troublesome to me.

If anger is red and shades of red on my color chart, then sad is blue. I see having a non happy day and feeling like doing anything is a drag as kind of a light sky blue. It travels into a midnight blue that says; life is unbearable and I want to die. Note that I said travels. There is a reason for that. It has been my experience that if I ignore sky blue, too often to suit me, it will become midnight blue. Thus, I say I have often added to the problem by the apathy I have shown concerning it.

The emotion itself is brought on by loss and is compounded by real or fancied feelings of inability to handle the loss. This can be anything from a problem with school to a change in realization about themselves. They lose something they thought they were. It brings a lack of interest and lack of energy, this in turn lowers the metabolism deepening the sadness and lowering yet further the metabolism. This is a simplistic way of saying it feeds off of itself. By knowing this, you can understand why my first choice is usually something that brings in activity and raises the metabolism.

As I have with all the other behaviors I strongly advise professional help if any child has continued ongoing signs of depression. Many of my consequences deal with handling behaviors, but are by no means a substitute for a professional. Some of these behaviors may even be signs of physical problems. Diabetes and hormone imbalance come to mind right off. Don't overlook those possibilities and do get the child to a doctor if the problem is prolonged.

NOTE: *Depression, in children, often is expressed as anger, irritability, or hostility.*

An interesting fact for what it is worth is that in young children, three to about nine, sadness often appears as hyperactivity. If you are experiencing some of those behaviors you might try treating them as sad behaviors and see if there is any noticeable change.

The bottom line with all sadness is to identify the loss, come to terms with the loss. Then form a plan for how to go on. So let us see what might help children do just that.

Tips To Remember:
1. Sadness says I have lost something and cannot deal with that loss.
2. Sadness feeds on itself if not dealt with. The more you ignore it the worse it gets.
3. Sadness deepens with lack of activity
4. Soft tones and insistence teach a sad person you believe in them, and that they can overcome.

Locks Self in Room

This is not the normal desire for privacy most children have but a prolonged time spent in their room with the door locked and when you call you get a GO AWAY type of message from them.

I would say any child spending over two hours per day, alone in their room is isolating.

These are for children that are *willing* to cooperate in consequences.

171. Come up with a plan. Limit the time in room and plan for the way child can use time constructively.
172. Manipulate the environment. Plan activities that will make the child unable to be in the room for a long time period.
173. Explain the dangers of the behavior and try to get child to participate in some high energy activity, catch, Frisbee, or a walk.
174. Insist they open door and you go into room. State that you are going to sit there for ten minutes and listen. Try to do just that. If they talk, outstanding, if they don't that's o.k. too
175. Put in a bedroom time. Such as you may be in your bedroom from 6:00 to 7:00 then at bedtime or for a specific reason; time out, change clothes.

These are for children that are *unwilling* to cooperate in consequences.

176. Take the lock off the door and allow them to earn it back by time spent with family or constructively.
177. After knocking, sit outside the door and pray aloud. Make sure to keep your voice tone gentle. When child asks what you are doing and they will, let them know when a problem is beyond your control you go to the power that can handle it. This also role models an answer to a problem they may have, so I like it.
178. You can place a handle with an auxiliary lock on the outside so you can get in. Assure child this is only so you can know that they are safe and because they will not let you in when you request it. This is a decision that will be better accepted at a **family meeting**.
179. If there is a real fear child may be hurting themselves pull the hinges and open the door. Basically this will make child feel less secure but when a real danger is there they must know you will protect them even from themselves.

ADD METHODS YOU HAVE USED:

_____
_____
_____
_____

Won't Talk

These are for children that are *willing* to cooperate in consequences.
180. Promise not to scold or consequent anything they say, offer just to listen. Ask if they would like some advise after they are done.
181. Share some experience you have gone through funny or embarrassing or related to current problem they are having. Let them know you may not have their answer but will be glad to listen.
182. Offer to go for a walk or a drive with them. Use silence to help them open up. Don't allow the radio to be on stating you would prefer to talk.
183. Have child sit in chair and just sit opposing them quietly assure them they can get up periodically but you need to talk about what is going on.
184. Let them know this is a hard thing for them to talk about and offer a reward after you have discussed it. I like chocolate or a sundae; it feels special.
185. Allow child to write you a letter to be discussed at a later time.

These are for children that are *unwilling* to cooperate in consequences.

186. Kneel down or position yourself to get eye contact with them then make a funny face. After a short time, assure them you'll stop if they will give you their name. Repeat the process asking for more information.
187. Withdraw all distractions, visitors, music, TV until the subject has been discussed.
188. Break it down into small pieces. Will you tell me what you had for lunch? Will you tell me what happened after that? Again, do not give advice or criticism to a child at this point. They will not hear it and it will only shut down communication even more.
189. Continue to bring subject up. If it is not critical allow them not to talk, wait half an hour bring it up, wait and bring it up again. A child will often talk if they know you will not let the issue die.
190. Make it into a game. Start a story about an imaginary person saying something like, "Little Johnny woke up this morning and then?" Allow the child to complete the sentence. This will help the child to start talking and may give you some insight into how they view the world.

ADD METHODS YOU HAVE USED:

_____
_____
_____
_____

Doesn't Do Chores

These are for children that are *willing* to cooperate in consequences.

191. Raise energy level by setting in an exercise program, explaining that it will help them have the strength to do their chores.
192. Make chore more fun—work it into a dance or singing routine.
193. Break it down into small pieces allowing a short break in between. 6:00 dishes off table, rest 2 minutes. 6:10 stack dishes.
194. Put in a pay rate in accordance with doing job. Well done, on time; without reminding, 75 cents. With reminding 50 cents, only half done after reminding, 25 cents. Note that this will only work if the lack of money puts some strain on the child. If you give them whatever they want it has no value.
195. Manipulate the environment by saying activity will be after chores, or placing chore time close to some other activity they enjoy.

These are for children that are *unwilling* to cooperate in consequences.

196. Simply do not do some chore that you are committed for, laundry, dinner, driving. When child is upset, explain this is how you feel when they do not do their chore. State you will attempt to be more responsible if they will.
197. Withdraw some normal given, shampoo, soda, snack, explaining from now on they will buy that with their chore money. Check your prices you may need to give them a raise.
198. At a **family meeting** bring up age appropriate responsibilities and privileges. Explain that the child's behavior makes you doubt they can handle that freedom and privileges will be cut accordingly. This needs to be for all family members if used.
199. Ignore the behavior but also ignore the reward. This works well for children who like to get into conflict with you. Be sure to give the reward to family members who are being responsible, including yourself.
200. Do their chore but charge them for it out of their allowance.

ADD METHODS YOU HAVE USED:
_____
_____
_____
_____

Won't Involve Self

We all have some things we prefer and some we are indifferent to. I speak here mostly of the child that throws cold water on all ideas presented to them and is a couch potato.

These are for children that are *willing* to cooperate in consequences.
201. At a **family meeting** confront the issue and force the child to look at and then pick some activity which they will participate in.
202. Have a code word with child that you can use to let the child know they are becoming uninvolved in an activity.
203. Continue to teach at every chance that involvement or the lack of it is a choice on the child's part. Many kids think that if they don't *feel* interested they can't *act* involved. Use life situations to point this out frequently.
204. Set a goal for the level of involvement you want for a child. Set time frames to reach each small part of the goal. One goal might be to be involved with a school activity and all family functions. By Friday the child will have checked on school activities available, by Sunday the child will have given at least one issue at a **family meeting**.
205. Use peers to motivate and add choices to the list. Invite peers over and discuss the type of things they do. Get child to commit to trying one for at least a month.

These are for children that are *unwilling* to cooperate in consequences.

206. Manipulate the environment. Plan activities in the house with the child's friend so they will be tempted to participate.
207. Call school counselor and set up a time for both of you to talk about an activity. Stress you are doing this because the child refuses to cooperate with you.
208. Withhold the TV or another item that fosters isolation. Again, stress this is because of child's unwillingness. Return it *as soon* as you get cooperation.
209. Pick a time and place the child in the front seat of the car and talk. Do not allow for distractions like the radio. Continue to confront the problem until you gain cooperation.

ADD METHODS YOU HAVE USED:

_____
_____
_____
_____

Poor School Grades

I want to make a short note here to remind ourselves that 'c' is average. Too often I hear parents expecting average kids to be exceptional and of course not all children are Einstein. That is something I thank God for every time I need a plumber. Be realistic in what you expect and what your child wants as far as employment goes!

These are for children that are *willing* to cooperate in consequences.
210. Set in a homework time daily. I prefer half an hour a day, before any other activity.
211. Have a school conference with teacher and go over daily or weekly grades and award privileges according to grades that day or week.
212. Get work sheets from teacher and give child added work daily. Do this only until grades improve otherwise you give the child the idea you are responsible for their grades, which of course you are not.
213. At a **family meeting** bring up grades and have some of the family talk about what motivates them.
214. Have child explore job market and what they will need educationally to meet their goals.
215. Sit with the child and try to hear their side of it. If a class is particularly unpleasant or their teacher difficult, find ways to improve the situation. You can often change the teacher.

These are for children that are *unwilling* to cooperate in consequences.

216. Set up weekly conferences with the teachers and the child and until an improvement is shown. Sometimes teachers are unable to do this, if so, set it up as often as possible. Be sure child is aware this will only go on until they are willing to cooperate in a plan of action.
217. Remove the TV until grades improve. If necessary put it in your room and allow other children to watch it. This can be a tricky one so try to remove it for the shortest time possible as child will quickly learn to amuse themselves without it. Push toward a homework time or tutor.
218. Place child with a tutor after school. Many schools offer a tutor program at school. If not, talk to teachers about using a neighborhood child who is doing well. Make child responsible for the cost of this by doing without snack or other extra.
219. Focus on the positive. Offer rewards and incentives for each improvement in grades. Bake a cake with the child's name on it. Or have everyone give them a round of applause at the **family meeting**. Do this for each small improvement rather the focusing on the whole grade. I had a child bring an 'F' to a 'B' by using only this.
220. Ignore the behavior but do not allow the child to not pay the price that the school puts in; summer school, special classes, or being held back.

ADD METHODS YOU HAVE USED:

_____
_____
_____

Won't Give Affection

This behavior is also a common control behavior when a child is irate. My personal belief is that everyone should have the right to not have to be affectionate to someone unless they want to, so I ignore that behavior. The behavior I am speaking of here is the child who consistently withholds any signs of affection and sometimes complains of touch hurting. This child will probably need therapy as well, for that is a sign of extreme depression or possibly former abuse.

These are for children that are *willing* to cooperate in consequences.
221. Set a plan with child for times when they feel the least threatened by being touched, in play, bedtime, then set in times for touch there.
222. Watch for times that child seems up and ask for hug or other sign of affection.
223. Do a study *with* child on the positive affects of touch. There are some surprisingly good books on that.
224. Sort through to the cause. See if the child is misreading what you are doing, or has picked up a faulty value.
225. Use play touch. Such as arm wrestling, patty cake and other games that require light touch. Point out that touch can feel safe and enjoyable. Again take care the touch is not hurtful and keep focusing on your goal.

These are for children that are *unwilling* to cooperate in consequences.

225. Tease touch, put your arms out and say you gave them a long distance hug anyway. Blow them a kiss. Show them affection can, but does not have to, include their participation.
226. Make comments like, I sure could use a hug then give yourself one. Keep the focus on touch being good but not a "you have to."
227. Role model touching. Let child know when whoever else is doing the touching, it makes you feel special and cared for. Let child tell you things that make them feel that way.
228. Move forward slowly. One night blow them a kiss. Night two kiss your hand, then place it on their cheek. Night three ask if you can kiss their hand goodnight. Night four ask if you can kiss them goodnight on the cheek. *Always ask permission* and be ready to accept no. Continue on at the level the child will accept.
229. Utilize bedtime stories and other free times to help child become aware that this is not how most people respond. Continue to feed the child information helping them come to grips with the problem. Try not to compare the child, simply pose questions.

ADD METHODS YOU HAVE USED:

_____
_____
_____
_____

Suicide Threats

This is another behavior I simply don't feel a parent can answer without a **trained professional**. This is a *dangerous behavior* in that, although the child could be trying to frighten you, it shows how their thinking could be life threatening. Therefore, everything I am giving you is a band-aid for a wound that needs stitches so to speak.

These are for children that are *willing* to cooperate in consequences.

230. Stop and immediately devise some intervention plan with child. Include such things as; then will you promise not to do that for a week, or until we can talk more about it. Let the child know it will be with someone who knows more than you do.
231. Have child call some help phone line whenever they feel that way. There are a number of such hot lines.
232. Set up an appointment with your minister and have them discuss life and death including the purpose for life. Be sure to be honest about what is going on.
233. Take child to a nursing home and let them talk to some of the people close to death.
234. Have them write reasons to live or get them to write about how different the world might have been without some hero who had a troubled past, I like Albert Einstein for a boy, or Helen Keller for a girl. The idea you want them to get is that trouble can strengthen us as well as overwhelm us.

These are for children that are *unwilling* to cooperate in consequences.

235. Start a bedtime reading of people who overcame problems in childhood and went on to greatness.
236. Remove all things that could be used to hurt themselves. Sharp toys, medicine, cleaning agents, knives.
237. Make a plan for checking on the child about every hour as to how they feel. Stress that they have you concerned and you need to be sure they are safe.
238. Do not allow them to go anywhere that they cannot be monitored until you are sure the mood is elevated. A good way to test that is to ask for ten reasons they like themselves and feel a part of the world today.
239. Accentuate the positive. Find at least ten things a day the child is doing right and you and others can make them aware of it.
240. Create a need or make the child aware of their being needed. I don't guess the dog would be here if not for you. After all who would love it and take care of it if you were gone?

ADD METHODS YOU HAVE USED:

_____
_____
_____
_____

Has No Friends

These are for children that are *willing* to cooperate in consequences.

241. Check child's social skills by planning a family activity with a new peer. Watch for things that might cause rejection then plan with child to overcome them.
242. Get them in a group activity and have them invite at least one person over a week. Again watch for behaviors that might cause them rejection.
243. Create a need. Go bowling and need a fourth person, need an extra to help prepare a cookout. Make child be responsible to ask a person to go. Be prepared to get that person there and back home.
244. Make friends with the parent of a child who lives close by. Set up a time to visit, both the parent and the child. Take your child with you. Be honest with your child about why you are taking them there.
245. Get child involved with youth activities. A church with a large membership in child's age group or a scout group or other activity. Give the child some choice in the activity they would prefer.

These are for children that are *unwilling* to cooperate in consequences.

246. Invite someone with a child that age over, being honest about your goal. Plan an activity for the children to do.
247. Call your local churches and see if they have youth that do missions. Explain your concerns and ask if they could call on your child.
248. Start a car pool in your neighborhood bringing kids to the lake, pool, or some other activity. Do not let your child get lost in the group. Pull them out by asking questions "How do you think about that or what would you like to see happen Johnny?"
249. Don't let them drop contact. Suggest calling back acquaintances made. Keep addressing the need for social contacts.
250. Identify the child's behavior and continue to show them when they have opportunities that they are missing to make a friend.

ADD METHODS YOU HAVE USED:

_____
_____
_____
_____

Doesn't Listen

These are for children that are *willing* to cooperate in consequences.

251. For the next hour make them repeat everything you say to them back to you, so you can be sure they heard you.
252. Have child come to you and make eye contact, then make your request. Keep this in effect until you are sure that they are more attuned to your voice.
253. Put your requests in writing for the next hour to a day and make sure that you give very little verbal interplay.
254. Have them go around and make the room quiet before you speak to them. Then talk to them.
255. Put up a chart and every time they hear you, give them a star. Keep the charts going for at least two weeks.

These are for children that are *unwilling* to cooperate in consequences.

256. Turn off all sound in the house for the next hour to make sure nothing drowns out the sound of your voice.
257. Go to them and make your voice tone very loud no matter what you are saying to them. Stress you will stop in an hour, or when they can assure you that they will hear you. Kids often perceive this as anger on your part, help them understand, it is simply how you handle people who are hard of hearing.
258. Don't talk to them at all for a while and when they ask why, in a loud voice tell them you didn't think they would hear you so why bother.
259. Go to the child make direct eye contact and slowly enunciate your words for about an hour. Start any statement with "Can you hear me?"

ADD METHODS YOU HAVE USED:
_____
_____
_____
_____

Hurting Self

In this behavior I am including all mild forms of self mutilation; the child who bites their nails to the quick. One who scratches their sores till they bleed or does some pulling out of their own hair. I *do not* mean a child who is severely slicing themselves, this child is suicidal, whether they verbalize it or not. I also am not speaking of the child that uses strangulation for a sexual high. This behavior is not suicidal although it can result in that and might respond to a take off on one of the behaviors I have listed in sexual behaviors. The serious forms are definitely ones you need to seek **professional help** for.

These are for children that are *willing* to cooperate in consequences.

260. Address the problem and let child know it is a behavior that upsets you because it can be harmful. Come up with a plan of what they can do instead.
261. Use band-aids, or another physical aid to make child aware when they are doing the behavior.
262. Have child stroke the area instead of picking. Use the same method with hair. With nails I have found chewing on an eraser often is a substitute that works.
263. Have child do a report on the possible outcomes of the behavior. This will be relatively hard for the child, but if you have "call a nurse" or some other health facility you can direct them to then you can use it.

These are for children that are *unwilling* to cooperate in consequences.

264. Focus on the solution. Every time you see the behavior point out it is harmful to them and offer an alternative.
265. Bring them to a medical facility and let a specialist inform them of the dangers involved with the behavior. You are wise to call in advance to let them know what you are trying to do.
266. Focus on the positive. When they are not picking a sore say "Your sore really is healing well you must not be picking it. That shows a lot of adult behavior and I am proud of you."
267. Use a reward. If the child has not bitten their nails for a few days buy them some nail polish, clear for boys and give them a manicure. Mouse or gel for hair. Skin creams for picking.
268. You can also remove such items from them until they start to show more responsibility caring for themselves. Again give them alternatives for the behavior.

ADD METHODS YOU HAVE USED:

_____
_____
_____
_____

Whining

These are for children that are *willing* to cooperate in consequences.

269. Address that the voice tone will not get what the child wants. Have child practice a more appropriate way of making a request.
270. Set in a whining time. Every day at 4:00 you must whine about things for ten to twenty minutes. You are not allowed to do anything else during that time, and you cannot whine at any other time. If child starts to whine, remind them to save it till 4:00.
271. Send child out of the room to allow them time to think about a better way of making request.
272. Do practice sessions on "no" and the proper response. This is one I like to address in a **family meeting**. If someone whines then they must practice having you say no five times and come up with different successful responses.
273. Address the issue of whining. Have the child start to list times they have whined and the results of that behavior. Ask if that is the result they are looking for this time.

These are for children that are *unwilling* to cooperate in consequences.

274. Ignore the behavior. Do not respond until the whining stops.
275. The next time child makes a request of you, whine. Let them know you will be responding that way to one of their requests each time they whine to one of yours.
276. Walk away the minute the whining starts. Return as soon as child stops. Do this with a lot of consistency if you use it, because it will probably take a number of times to get what you want.
277. Stop what you are doing and cover your ears. Do not uncover them until the voice tone returns to normal.
278. Sing or hum, let the child know you are trying to not listen to that tone of voice.

ADD METHODS YOU HAVE USED:

_____
_____
_____
_____

Sexual Behavior, the Shocking Mask

I often think of this behavior as a brightly colored purple mask. The behavior draws such attention to itself, that what lies beneath that behavior often remains undiscovered. Like all other behavior colors this one shades from the pale lavender which might be off color jokes to the vivid chartreuse of rape. I have not addressed either fetishes or rape because I honestly am not sure how I would successfully handle those. I do know I would contact a **specialist in the field** and at the same time modify some of these consequences to fit the behavior.

This behavior finds its roots in a number of places. It can be *a sign that sexual abuse has occurred*, especially if this behavior is found in a child under thirteen. Wisdom needs to be used here and we need to stress strongly that you bring your child **to a specialist**. However, many adolescents fall into sexual behaviors as a way of finding acceptance in their peer group. Others find it a source of power. I can get what I want through sexual behavior. Still others have not got the stamina or assertiveness to take a firm stand. The last group of children are those who have sexual needs that they haven't learned how to deal with. Like all things the emotion behind the behavior is the thing you need to get to and redirect.

The hardest thing to remember is human sexuality is *good* and there to keep mankind going. When a child is very young and these behaviors start, I want to whitewash it and not address the issues. Experience has found this is *not good*. If the child is engaging in sexual behavior no matter what the age, the need is for non-judgmental, factual information. They also need clear boundaries or limits. This can become difficult especially if you are not sure what your limits are. Any parent who is experiencing these behaviors with their child should first sit down with a pencil and paper and write with whom, how far, how soon, where, and what protection. Now re-look at that and look at your own life experiences and those of your friends. Do they come anywhere near matching? If they don't, revamp it to make it more realistic. If you come across as the saint, your child will disregard you entirely. Better you get some achievable boundaries then none.

Tips to remember:
1. Sexual behaviors in children **can be a sign of sexual abuse**.
2. Human sexuality is God given and therefore good.
3. This behavior is usually a mask that hides another need.
4. Non judgmental facts are usually best received by child.
5. Inventory what you want, whether it is realistic or not.

Sneaking Out

This is a behavior that usually is peer connected. For that reason I have found it most effective to pull peers into the consequence.

These are for children that are *willing* to cooperate in consequences.

279. Stop contact with anyone who was involved in the episode for at least two weeks. Slowly allow the companion around first while in your home together. Then short periods of time alone together.
280. Have them do an essay on the number of children found hurt that were not where they were supposed to be. The story of Sharon Shafer although rather gruesome, is quite informative. Go over the essay together showing your concern for child.
281. Have child compile a list of every friend, with phone number and address and parent's name that they know. Inform them that next time each one of these people will be contacted.
282. For the next two weeks have child call you every half hour to build back some of the trust they lost.
283. Show you're upset and that you spent the time they were gone worried and now you need to rest. Have child pick up your responsibilities for the day.
284. Listen in on phone call from friends for the next week until you can assure yourself they are not talking about sneaking out.
285. Have the child go over where they were and why. Call and verify if possible. Form a safe alternative in case the situation happens again.
286. Run away with them. Form a pact that they can run away, but only if they tell you first. Then when they say they are going to run say great let me pack a few things. Inform the family you are running away and go somewhere, talk and help the child come to the decision to go back home.

These are for children that are *unwilling* to cooperate in consequences.

287. Call the police. When child returns have the police come to the house to talk to them.
288. Call every peer and person you know ask if they have seen the child. Make child responsible to explain this behavior to these people.
289. Remove the telephone, explaining that you are not sure they won't use it to plan another such outing. Return it as a reward for no more sneaking out. I usually say one week, but if they do it again I assure them it will be two weeks.
290. Make it an issue. For the next couple of weeks whenever you run into one of their friends ask if they know where the child was, spend about two minutes recounting your fear. Get the people's assurance they will let you know if they see the child out without you.
291. Offer the child a choice. They can run away and you will not call the police, but only if they call you every hour to let you know they are safe. This works and takes much of the excitement out of running away.

ADD METHODS YOU HAVE USED:

_____
_____
_____
_____

Wrong Friends

This becomes somewhat tricky because to forbid them to see their friends not only sets you up as a parent as controlling, it often takes you out of the position of helping a child learn to make good choices about their friends. For this reason I try very hard to stay focused on behaviors.

These are for children that are *willing* to cooperate in consequences.
292. Hold a **family meeting** and get the family's impression of the friend. Have them share how child acts while around the friend. Allow child to explore the impact of the friend on his life.
293. Have your child get details about their friend, including how much trouble they have gotten into in school, at home, and with the authorities. List your concerns and allow the child to come up with a plan to not put themselves in danger of being caught in one of those entanglements.
294. Have child write a list of the pro's and the cons for continuing the friendship. Allow them the choice but only under supervised conditions.
295. Have child list the reasons why they chose this friend. Look closely at this with child sorting out which of these reasons are valid.
296. Come to a compromise. Let your child know you do not approve of their choice but you are willing to take a chance if contact is under controlled conditions. At your house, at school, and other closely supervised events.

These are for children that are *unwilling* to cooperate in consequences.

297. Go to the friend and be clear about your concerns and the behaviors that worry you. Have the friend come up with a plan for more acceptable behaviors while with your child.
298. Be a mother hen. Stay underfoot when the friend is around. Call and check that they are where they are supposed to be. Assure your child that it is their choice in friends rather than their behavior that is bringing this on.
299. Manipulate the environment. Every time the friend calls or comes over have something that your child needs to do.
300. Offer a choice. I wouldn't mind you going skating with Joey, but I just don't feel safe when you are with Tom so you can go skating with Joey or stay here with Tom.
301. Ignore the friend and wait for wrong behavior. But share your concerns right off. When the behavior occurs point out the behavior and limit all contact with friend to supervised contact.

ADD METHODS YOU HAVE USED:

_____
_____
_____
_____

Dresses Inappropriate

I would like to comment here that fashions change and what was scandalous in our mother's era is modest now. Some outfits are not appropriate for the setting. You must be the judge, but take into account current fashions and your children's need to feel accepted.

These are for children that are *willing* to cooperate in consequences.

302. Sit with your child and negotiate a compromise. If you will wear this to church I will let you wear that to the ball game.
303. Set the ground rules before the game. You can have that outfit but, the only places you can wear it is around the house.
304. Get a group conscience. Ask the other members of the family how it makes the child appear to them. Then tell child you are going with the majority vote.
305. Just say "no". Tell child they can wear it, but if they do they cannot go to wherever they are headed.
306. Reason it out. Talk to your child and try to find out why the desire for this type of clothing. Come up with other ways to fill that need.
307. Call in outside help. Have the child call three people in three age groups and let the overriding opinion rule. The child may end up wearing the outfit, but it will communicate that the choice takes extra time and trouble.

These are for children that are *unwilling* to cooperate in consequences.

308. Ignore the behavior for the moment and at a later time take the article of clothing. If the clothing is appropriate in another setting, return the article when you see cooperation.
309. Explain to the child that the outfit makes you concerned for what they will be doing and if they insist on wearing it you will be forced to accompany them.
310. Assure them they can wear it but...if they are old enough to disregard your wishes they are old enough to buy their own clothes. Be careful on this one "because it has backfired when I had a child do just that and had to accept it. It backfired another time when I couldn't follow through."
311. Allow the outfit, but give no attention to the child while they are wearing it. Explain that it embarrasses you to be with them when they are dressed like that. Counter that with lavish attention when they make the right choice.
312. Refuse to be a cooperative party in them dressing like that. Don't drive them, let them use the phone, or greet their friends, if they insist on wearing the outfit.

ADD METHODS YOU HAVE USED:

_____
_____
_____
_____

Making Advances

When I speak of making advances as a misbehavior I am assuming that the person they are making the advances on is not appropriate, or the child is too young, or the place is wrong. Sometimes children come up with a faulty opinion of what is acceptable to others and this is what I concentrate on teaching.

These are for children that are *willing* to cooperate in consequences.

313. Sit with child and go over what the exact movements are that are giving the sexual message. Plan a time when child can practice using different skills. One afternoon a week for two weeks works well for me.
314. Have them go to one of the model agency promotions and bring up the behavior they are displaying. These are free and the models teach **great** value lines.
315. If problem is verbal spend ten to fifteen minutes a day having child share why and what they feel is the outcome they want from this. At the end of the week review it with child and help them see if they are really getting what they want or if they couldn't find a healthier way to get it.
316. Have a **family meeting** or get a group of the child's peers together and discuss haw the behavior makes them feel.
317. Delay time with opposite sex until they can show better interaction. Another way to do that is make the first three times they wish to be with someone, at your home, so you are sure they are not rushing things.

1001 NATURAL LOGICAL CONSEQUENCES

These are for children that are *unwilling* to cooperate in consequences.

318. Confront the behavior. Let child know that it makes you and others feel threatened or invaded. Do that with some consistency.
319. Approach the other party involved directly in the presence of the child and apologize for the behavior. Ask the other person if they would mind honestly sharing how that makes them feel.
320. Set firm limits. If I see you do this behavior I will not take you back to this place for two weeks.
321. Along the same lines as above you can say if this person has that affect on you I will ask them not to come around again. With either of these you will need to move toward "why are you doing this and does it work?"
322. Pre-teach. I will take you with me but only if I have your word there will be no advances made on some unsuspecting person while we are out. This works well with kids that are caught in power plays.

ADD METHODS YOU HAVE USED:

_____
_____
_____
_____

Caught Having Sex

This is an embarrassing behavior for all people involved. I have had the experience and all I wanted to do was close the door and not address it. I feel the first part of the judgment call was right. All these are better addressed after the fact. I speak only for myself when I say I have never successfully stopped a child from having sex. I can also say I have had almost all of my children make a choice to leave sex alone until they were better equipped to handle it. I have done this by continuing to focus on what the behavior is giving them and are they willing to pay the possible high price to meet that need.

These are for children that are *willing* to cooperate in consequences.

323. Set a time aside and privately address the issue. Speak clearly of what you expect in terms of protection and places where this could be appropriate in happening. Build a game plan for what is to occur next.
324. Have child go through a health and safety routine where sexual behaviors are concerned, make them relate what measures they took to insure that. Did they use protection, was the other person tested for HIV+ first, do they know the other person's sexual history, and things of that nature. Ask their plan of action if the worst occurs.
325. Bring them to a clinic and have them checked for disease. Have nurses relate at the clinic some of the problems they have seen with youthful sex.
326. Sit with both parties and talk of their plans, responsibilities, and where they plan on going from that point.
327. Offer alternatives: masturbation, keeping themselves in places where the act becomes impossible, strenuous activities. I offer cold showers, but personally the only person they seemed to make feel better was my mother.
328. Get a book on sexual behaviors the choices and consequences of those behaviors. Have your child read it and discuss it with them.

These are for children that are *unwilling* to cooperate in consequences.

329. Break all private contact until you get mature behavior. In other words their unwillingness tells you they are not ready to handle the freedom of being alone with the partner or any other likely candidate.
330. Go to the other child involved. Explain you want certain things of them before they can be alone with your child again. Ask for a medical exam and a **written** statement of what they plan on assuming responsibility for and how they plan on doing it.
331. Go to your child's friends and ask for their limits where sexual matters are concerned. Get their opinion of others who don't hold true to that value. Bring this information to your child. Before doing this, make it very clear what your plans are, and that it is because the child won't work with you that you are forced to take this action. Keep your tone open and non judgmental. Give them a chance to cooperate.
332. Use spiritual aids. Have child go to a minister or other spiritual teacher and be honest. Get the viewpoint of the church regarding the matter. Many churches have some exceptional literature on this type of thing.

ADD METHODS YOU HAVE USED:

_____
_____
_____
_____

Public Masturbation

This is a behavior that many specialists in the field seem to give as an indication of **sexual abuse**. If you have not seen someone who is qualified to make that judgment we **strongly suggest you seek a professional**. All I am dealing with here is the behavior and some possible ways of handling it. If the problem goes deeper, you will need to **seek professional help** for the answer. From six months to about three years old this is common and normally acceptable behavior.* The only thing you need to do is teach privacy.
  According to some child care experts.

These are for children that are *willing* to cooperate in consequences.

333. Take child aside and explain the where's and how's of their own body (their body belongs to them and some things may feel good, also no one has a right to touch them in certain places etc). Make them aware that when they do that in front of people they make others uncomfortable. Give them a plan of action, and places they could masturbate without upsetting others.
334. Watch for time periods. If it is occurring at a given time make that time spent in the privacy of their own room daily.
335. Sit down with the child and preplan behaviors. If it seems to be impulsive or a thing they are almost unaware they are doing, give them a code word that will make them aware and something else to do with their hands.
336. Teach them cat's cradle or another string and hand type movement game. Have them carry that in their pocket and play it whenever they are in a locale where masturbation is likely to occur.

These are for children that are *unwilling* to cooperate in consequences.

337. State that behavior is offensive to you and leave the room. Bring anyone else who is present with you and shut off any entertainment. Wait about five minutes and return asking if the person is finished.
338. Refuse to take child with you to family gatherings or public places until the behavior is addressed and an alterative is implemented. Try to keep you voice tone and words non judgmental and stay focused on the privacy issue.
339. Do not allow the child to lay out in living room, but instead have them sit in a straight back chair with the chair turned backwards. This positioning makes masturbation almost impossible and keeps child aware. When I use this it is as a teaching method of helping child be aware they have a choice. It also assumes this is where the behavior is occurring.
340. Insist on proper behavior before you take child anywhere. Once you have the child's word then pre-teach that (you will go home the minute such behavior occurs), and follow through on it.
341. If the behavior is happening away from you, for example, in school, or at a friend's, either take away the privilege of going from the child for the day, or go with the child for a day. Use the one that works in the given situation.
342. Set up a Physicians appointment and address the problem honestly with the Doctor. Make sure there is no physical reason, then have the doctor go over some alternatives.

ADD METHODS YOU HAVE USED:

_____
_____
_____

Sexual Language

This is often no more than attention getting behavior, so I have made the consequences small. I am inclined to focus more on the people this behavior is occurring around than the behavior itself because it is often used by peers.

These are for children that are *willing* to cooperate in consequences.

343. Have child write five other ways they could have verbalized what they were saying more appropriately.
344. Have the child look up the words in the dictionary and stating the true meaning, say why they said that and if it is a true statement. For example if they say (F**** You) Have them look the words up and explain why they would want to have intercourse with you.
345. Form a plan of action with the child. See what the child wants from the behavior and offer them another way to get it. I wanted them to notice me *can be re-formed* into "Hi you sure look pretty today."
346. Take away the privilege of doing whatever they were doing for the day. Explain that kind of talk shows they need to work on their verbal skills more before they are ready for that privilege.

1001 NATURAL LOGICAL CONSEQUENCES

These are for children that are *unwilling* to cooperate in consequences.

347. Address the problem in a **family meeting** and have the other members relate how they would have preferred child state it.
348. Refuse to respond to anything but written communication for the next half an hour.
349. Ignore the behavior and reward the positive behavior. Say nothing about the sexual remark, but whenever child is positive, give lots of verbal reinforcement saying how you like it much better, and how it appears more adult than the old behavior.
350. Go to the other person involved and apologize for the behavior in front of the child. Say it is rude and immature and that you are trying to get them to look at it as such.
351. Reword the sentence yourself for the child and repeat it back to them. Continue to do this whenever the language is used. Assure the child you will stop doing that when the child is willing to work on the behavior, but you must assume that they need to learn more positive communication skills so you are role modeling for them.

ADD METHODS YOU HAVE USED:

_____
_____
_____
_____

Exposing Self

This is a behavior that is mostly done for shock value. It gets attention and has its own sort of naughty thrill. If it is not stopped by consequences, we *strongly recommend* taking the child to a **child therapist** as this may signal **sexual abuse**. But if it is for simple shock value a lot of this will stop if the consequences do not give much in the way of attention.

These are for children that are *willing* to cooperate in consequences.
352. Tell the child that is unacceptable and have them put on an extra article of clothing. Tell them it will help them remember.
353. Have the child sort through why they did that. Ask them to come up with three alternatives.
354. Have child state the body part and the appropriate use for it. Reinforce that, and then have them explain why it is not appropriate to expose themselves. If they can't explain have them find out why.
355. Have child wear overalls or some other article of clothing that in difficult to remove for the rest of the day.
356. Have child find scripture or other literature on the expectations of society in the matter of covering ones body.

These are for children that are *unwilling* to cooperate in consequences.

357. Ignore the behavior. The next time you are going out refuse to take child because you are not sure they can act appropriately.
358. Ignore the behavior and insist on choosing clothing that is not easy to expose themselves in the next time you go out.
359. The next time you go clothes shopping limit their choices to clothing that is hard to expose themselves in. Stress that this is due to their lack of co-operation in this matter.
360. Remove all clothing that is easy access from their closet and have them earn it back with every hour of not exposing themselves. This can be very effective, but be careful because it is also easy for you to box yourself in because your child has to have clothes.
361. Take bed time stories or T.V. time away and replace it with Bible stories or literature dealing with modesty. You read it to the child so they cannot manipulate and not read it. Also make sure it comes out of time already being spent with them in an enjoyable way.

ADD METHODS YOU HAVE USED:

_____
_____
_____
_____

Playing with Feces

This is a behavior common in, but not limited to younger children. One of the age considerations you must make as a parent is the degree of privacy the child is entitled to. Any of these consequences that have *you* in the bathroom with the child should not be used with a child over seven.

These are for children that are *willing* to cooperate in consequences.

362. Have child clean it up using plastic gloves. Also have them clean the surrounding area.
363. Have child ask permission to go to the bathroom for the next week. Check the room after they are done.
364. If the behavior is occurring in the child's room, put the child on a bathroom schedule. They must go to the bathroom at certain times and must try to go. Reward them going. Do check to make sure they have gone.
365. Give them alternatives. Play dough or bread dough works well. Make a chart that will show three to five days of not playing with feces gets the reward of using the play dough.
366. Have the child call a local heath official and find out why that behavior has health issues. Have them bring the information to the family in the **family meeting**.

These are for children that are *unwilling* to cooperate in consequences.

367. Use the **family meeting** to confront the issue and have other family members point out why they do not do this.
368. Monitor the bathroom time. Using it appropriately earns the next time unsupervised, but checked afterwards. If that time it is clean, try not checking again. You may have to repeat this process several times, but the goal is to get them to where you don't have to check the bathroom after them.
369. Sit the child down and go over the health issues involved. Withdraw all privileges until the child has cleaned up after themselves.
370. Act disgusted. Refuse to allow child near you until they have bathed. Stress the behavior causes a health hazards to all members of the family.

ADD METHODS YOU HAVE USED:

_____
_____
_____
_____

Wrong Care of Sanitary Napkins

These are for children that are *willing* to cooperate in consequences.

371. If the misuse is too many or playing with them, make the child responsible for the cost above the normal amount.
372. If the misuse is in disposal or displaying them, have child go through a practice session showing you what she should be doing with them.
373. Have her call a plumber and ask for cost of unblocking a toilet and start a collection toward the probable expense. Stop this when you see the appropriate care.
374. Take the choice away of what she uses, if she uses tampons switch to pads or visa-versa. Explain you feel that this might encourage proper use. Allow choice when you get appropriately behavior.

1001 NATURAL LOGICAL CONSEQUENCES

These are for children that are *unwilling* to cooperate in consequences.

375. Keep the pads in your room, only allow another when you have been shown proper disposal of the one used previously. Do this for only short term as it really is a lot of monitoring.
376. Do not allow for the use of bathrooms outside the home during menstrual cycle. Assure the girl you will be glad to allow this privilege again as soon as you get co-operation on the disposal of pads.
377. Make a chart and account for all the pads and the disposal of them or use of them. Have her be accountable for the overage. If she is unwilling to reimburse you, simply take away an item of equal value, snacks, or a favorite hair care item works well for me.
378. Buy the most inexpensive brand. Be sure to let the girl know her use of them makes you have to plan money differently. Also assure her that right behavior will get the favored type back.

ADD METHODS YOU HAVE USED:
_____
_____
_____
_____

Touching or Hugging Sexually

When I speak of this I am talking about the child who makes you, or others uncomfortable with the way they hug or touch you. Fundamentally, they misuse the right for affection by turning it into a sexual act, or at least it *feels* that way.

These are for children that are *willing* to cooperate in consequences.
379. Call the child's attention to the behavior immediately. Have them practice a more appropriate way of hugging.
380. Bring the issue up in a **family meeting** and have the other members of the family share how the behavior makes them feel.
381. Make a chart listing all the touching and have child rate himself to others, how comfortable are they with child's touch; as in person's name, type of touch, made them feel. Offer a reward for a week of nothing but comfortable touches.
382. Have child state type of touching and ask permission before the action. I would like to give you a hug would you mind?
383. Have child cut the time spent touching in half. If they are hanging and petting on people say, "You can touch the person, but then you must withdraw your hand." I find giving the child a number to count to helps concrete that behavior. "When you count to three your hand should no longer be on the other person."

These are for children that are *unwilling* to cooperate in consequences.

384. Confront the behavior. Move away from the child and state that you do **NOT** like being touched in that manner. Refuse any physical contact for the next couple of hours reinforcing your feelings.
385. Pre-teach the desired behavior by physically moving away when child approaches you and ask them to tell you what they want and then give them the behavior you want. "Yes you can put your arm around me, but do not go near my breast."
386. If the behavior is happening with others do not allow unsupervised time with others until you see the proper behavior; stress that you will allow them to be alone with others only if they can touch appropriately.
387. Confront the behavior with the others involved. "When Johnny rubs you like that it makes me uncomfortable, how does it make you feel?" Assure the other person they have the right to ask the child not to touch them.
388. Physically distance yourself or others from the child by moving out of the range of touch. Build in other ways of expressing affection such as notes, verbal comments. Only do this for limited times, *human beings need appropriate touch.*

ADD METHODS YOU HAVE USED:

_____
_____
_____
_____

Has Pornographic Literature

It is my personal feeling that much of this behavior is typical teenage curiosity. I do realize it is illegal and in many cases distasteful to parents. Because the best we can do is hope to control it in our home I have avoided any consequences that form major power struggles I cannot hope to win.

These are for children that are *willing* to cooperate in consequences.

389. Have the child do a study on the legal consequences of the behavior. Focus it on what could happen to the person who gave them the literature.
390. Have them write an essay on what it must feel like to be considered valuable only for your body. Try to get them to see themselves in that light and what would their worth be?
391. Make them burn the literature. This is a good way of concreting a commitment not to have any more.
392. Have them do a short study on the opposite sex's opinion of how it would feel to have a partner who was into pornographic literature.
393. Get some alternative educational books, maybe appropriate books about "A teenager's changing body". Pornography can have a lot of perversion, so you might want to suggest some healthy ways to look at sex.

These are for children that are *unwilling* to cooperate in consequences.

394. Take the literature. Tell the child they are not of a legal age to have it and you will not allow it in your house.
395. Start a room search. It needs to be clear to the child they lost the privilege of privacy when they brought contraband articles in.
396. Explain the reason you object to pornography. Allow for resistance, but share your experience and reason for your feelings on the matter. Try very hard to be factual, rather than judgmental.
397. Bring the child to a minister or a counselor of the same sex that the child can talk freely to. Tell the person what your concerns are in front of the child and then leave.
398. Find out where they got the material. If the child will not tell you, start calling their friends, do not make a secret of what you are doing as this will encourage honesty. Once you know where they got it, inform the person involved that you do not want your child to have any further literature like that, and make them aware that it is a criminal offence. Try not to be too hard on the other person since this is a good opportunity to build trust with your own child.

ADD METHODS YOU HAVE USED:

_____
_____
_____
_____

Making Sexual Gestures

When I speak of sexual gestures I refer mainly to suggestive movements of the hips, sticking their tongue out and other lewd type of behavior. Although giving someone the finger is a sexual gesture its meaning is usually angry. I am more inclined to use other angry type consequence but some of these can work for that as well.

These are for children that are *willing* to cooperate in consequences.

399. Have the child clarify what they meant by that in writing and list some of the probable outcomes.
400. Explore the options. Ask the child why they behaved in such a manner and try to get them to see if it is really getting them what they want.
401. Come up with a plan for other more opposite ways to get the desired message across. Have the child practice them with you.
402. Tell the child to act out three more appropriate responses they could have used.
403. Have them write five to ten times I will not act in this manner.
404. Have them count to ten before they talk to anyone for the next fifteen minutes to an hour. Explain that this is to help them be less impulsive.

These are for children that are *unwilling* to cooperate in consequences.

405. Ask the next three people you both come into contact with how they would feel if this behavior was done to them.
406. Refuse to take the child to wherever the episode occurred next time. Allow them to have it the time after that by not acting in that manner.
407. Parrot the behavior that you want five to ten times. Assure the child you will no longer need to do that once they are willing to cooperate in solving the problem.
408. Use humor. Post a sign **DANGER** RUDE AND LEWD COMMENTS MAY BE EXPERIENCED IN HERE! ENTER AT YOUR OWN RISK!!! Post it on their door but suggest if the behavior continues it might need to be posted in a more public place. Do keep this on a light note or the child may engage in a power struggle and give you more of the behavior than before.
409. Ignore the behavior. At a later time when one of the child's friends visits, casually remark should you greet them with the gesture that they used since it seems to be a new way of meeting people. If you are very brave you can even do this. I have found it does have quite an impact on children. I always clean up the shock afterwards by laughing and explaining to the child that we have an inside joke. Always assure your child that they can control your behavior if they will role model the right behavior to you.

ADD METHODS YOU HAVE USED:

_____
_____
_____
_____

Fear of Opposite Sex

There is always a certain amount of this in teens, both male and female encounters. If I have a child who goes to long lengths to avoid contact with the opposite sex I am inclined to assume there is a problem. During the teenage years I feel that kids are in danger of making poor choices if they don't feel equipped to make acceptable ones.

These are for children that are *willing* to cooperate in consequences.
410. Address the problem. Talk as honestly as possible about the child's concerns. Get books or a professional to come up with some concrete answers.
411. Role model the behavior you want. Point out to the child the interaction when you are with the opposite sex. Make the child aware of how you set the limits.
412. Break it down into small steps for the child and set some goals. I will say hi to a person of the opposite sex on the school bus today. Tomorrow I will ask about a class they are in. Be sure to help child read the messages the other person is giving.
413. Get them to share their concerns with a person of the opposite sex whom you trust. Have that person share the things they liked and didn't like with that area.
414. Make a game of it. Act silly around a peer of the opposite sex the child knows and have the child apologize for you. You can also give your child an opening to meet those of the opposite sex in a more subtle way with the same results.

These are for children that are *unwilling* to cooperate in consequences.

415. Utilize an older brother or sister or another teen that you are comfortable with. Share what is going on and ask them to help the child understand some of the feelings that are going on with the opposite sex. Try to sit in on this if you use it. Unfortunately, I have found the older peer often is confused and can pass that on. If you can't be there, have the older child talk to you first and you pretend to be the younger child.
416. Manipulate the surroundings. Put the child in situations where there is a child of the opposite sex and they are pretty much forced to interact. Plan an activity that will help them not feel lost in this venture.
417. Go to the school guidance counselor and explain your concerns. See if the child could act as a tutor or in some other capacity that would place them in a position to get to know peers of the opposite sex.
418. Give lots of praise and reinforcement. I have found that most of these kids really fear rejection. The more you can assure them that someone might accept them and can point out why, the better.

ADD METHODS YOU HAVE USED:

_____
_____
_____

The Little Princess, Careless Behavior

I always see this behavior as different shades of yellow. This is because in my mind, I equate it to happy go lucky, carefree, type of behaviors; pale yellow being almost a white and hardly worth noticing—A book left for you to pick up, or a chore poorly done. The brightest shade a glaring yellow that burns your eyes even to look at—Property destroyed, and no remorse even felt or maybe people treated as if they had neither feelings nor value.

Below the behavior, as with all the others, stands a basic need. I think it is self-worth. Although twisted up, it really is the belief that I am important and worthy. Unfortunately, when it has been cultivated wrongly it tells us one giant lie; it tells us that we are the only ones whose rights we need concern ourselves with. The even sadder truth is that many times, as a parent, I have cultivated the very weeds that now choke me. How? By being very responsible myself, not taking the added time to insist that the child does their part or pays the price. By being very loving and in saying this time doesn't count. Of course it does count...as one more time that other person need not be regarded when the child has a desire to do something.

To me, at the heart of this behavior should be the ability to teach the child that others are as important as they are. The first step in that always appears to be *allowing* the child to feel the *discomfort* of their own thoughtlessness. Once that has happened they are more inclined to want to consider others and then learn the benefits of being responsible.

One of the easiest pitfalls for me to fall into is killing their own feeling of self worth. I don't wish to teach them they are not important, simply that others are just as important. It is easy to understand how one could misread the message we parents give once we understand that children have a lifetime belief that some people are princesses, while others are slaves. If mom no longer considers me the princess than I guess I'm the slave. I watch for signs of that happening. Some of the signs of this are a disinterest in their own pleasures, becoming overly concerned with doing for others, or a surge of feeling used or victimized.

My rule of thumb for this is: would it seem right if I were in the other guy's shoes? When I approach it this way I can almost always find a happy medium.

Tips to remember:
1. Carelessness has its roots in self worth.
2. Your child needs to learn there are no princes/princesses, nor are there any slaves.
3. Before they can realize the benefits of being responsible they seem to need to experience the pain of being irresponsible.
4. Look out for signs that your child is losing their own sense of self worth.
5. If I can "put the shoe on the other foot," chances are good; I can see what is fair.

Doesn't Pick Up

These are for children that are *willing* to cooperate in consequences.

419. Have the child go back and pick up the article plus three other things of someone else's. Explain that is how others feel when forced to pick up their things.
420. Have the child pick up article and write or tell you why they should not leave it laying around.
421. Have child pick up the room the article is in along with picking up the article.
422. Make the room off limits to the child for the next hour, explaining they have misused it therefore must not be ready for the right of it. When you allow them in the room make them pick up the article.
423. Have a day off for the people who have picked up after themselves. The ones who haven't are required to do the chores that day. You will probably need a chart for this. If all members of the family have a perfect week, allow one day where no one cleans the house.
424. Have the child who doesn't pick up be Mom for a day and leave your things around. Have them try to convince you to pick them up.
425. Get a child's teaching book on responsibility, such as Bern hart Bears. Have them read it aloud every time they leave something out. Ask them who they want to be like. Have the child decide which behavior they want.

These are for children that are *unwilling* to cooperate in consequences.

426. Pick up the article and require the child to buy it back. Do this by offering to let them earn it back with one of the above or you will take it out of their earned money or snacks. Stress that they are choosing to pay you for maid service when they leave things around.
427. Ignore the behavior and the article and when they request something of you assure them they can have it as soon as they pick their item up. This is probably my favorite, it teaches inconveniencing me—inconveniences them. It takes a little time but I have never gotten caught in a struggle of wills with it.
428. Confiscate the article for a week. Have a box where you keep them and only give them back once a week. The effectiveness of this depends on the value of the article to the child. Sunday shoes to you might represent a loss that the child considers a gain because it allows them to wear sneakers to church. Measuring the importance will help you see when it will be the most effective.
429. Hide the article. Be clear with the child that you assumed that it had little value to them and so you can raise its value by making something they put some effort into. The child needs to find the article to gain possession of it. As with the above the value to the child will determine the effectiveness.
430. Delay some privilege that you were going to give. Tell the child that you have spent the energy you would have used to do this on picking up after them and now you need to rest. Assure the child that he or she can help you gain this energy by doing something for you.

ADD METHODS YOU HAVE USED:

_____
_____
_____

Steals Property

This is a behavior that is illegal as well as inconsiderate. I personally like a consequence that teaches the legal aspects as well as the emotional ones.

These are for children that are *willing* to cooperate in consequences.
431. Have the child return the property to the manager of the store and apologize to them.
432. Have the child go to the store face the manager and make financial restitution for the value of the property.
433. Have the child write a letter of apology for the manager and include the amount of the item and mail it to the manger. I will use this on a child who is willing but very resistant of face to face contact.
434. Have the child donate the cost of the item to the poor and do a report or tell you the legal dangers in theft. I use this when I cannot discover where the article came from, or cannot contact the person to return the article.
435. Call the police. Have them confront the child and explain the penalties of theft. Set in similar penalties at home or pick one of them, such as community hours (i.e. Community Service), and have child do them.
436. Have the child give the article to the police and do a confession.

ADD METHODS YOU HAVE USED:

_____
_____
_____
_____

These are for children that are *unwilling* to cooperate in consequences.

437. Confiscate the article. The next time you are out with the child walk into the store call the manager and tell them what has happened apologizing for the child. Do **NOT** tell the child what you are planning to do. If the child runs out of the store finish what you are doing. Relate what happened and the owner's response in as calm a manner as you can.

438. Confiscate an item of equal value. Make the store where the item was taken (or a family member's room) off limits until the child is willing to make some sort of apology.

439. Call the police. Have them explain the court system and penalties for theft. Give the child a choice to participate in one of the penalties or go through the process of pressing charges. Be careful on this one to make sure you are willing to follow through if your child chooses the court system. I have found it to be time consuming and not always the outcome I expected.

440. If it is a home theft place a lock on the other parties' door. Take an article of equal or greater value and give it to the victim.

441. Withdraw all shopping privileges until you get an oral or verbal report on the probable outcome of a thief and why. Include some form of restitution.

442. If the theft is at home or food articles, take the amount of snacks deserts and sodas that you would give the child and divide it amount the other family members. Make sure the child is aware they are losing a greater amount than what they took.

443. Another very effective way to control home theft is to give the offender the lesser cost items such as oatmeal without sugar or mush for breakfast. At the same time use the saved money to give the victim a high cost favorite cereal. You might want to keep the high cost cereal in your room.

Won't Return Things

These are for children that are *willing* to cooperate in consequences.

444. Set in a *house rule* at a **family meeting** that there will be a late fine for anything not returned before due date. Keep a pencil and pad ready so everyone can mark down item borrowed and date due for return.
445. Talk with child on the liabilities of lateness. Have the child write down the probable costs of that type of behavior. Put it on their wall and get a commitment to return things on time.
446. Have the child write five to ten times I will return items on time.
447. For the next two weeks do not allow any borrowing, explaining that the child has broken your trust by the lateness.
448. Have the child return everything for the next week after only half the time they were allotted. An example would be a child asks to borrow a pencil for an hour. You say yes but in half an hour they must return it to you and ask someone else to borrow one. Their other choice is to borrow it for two hours and have it back in one. Both work because both teach time management and responsibility.
449. If the problem is borrowing from friends, make a *house rule* nothing comes in the house that does not belong to the child without your permission. Insist that the child let you make the negotiations with any person they are borrowing from. After that you can proceed with any of the above.
450. Have the child only be able to borrow things by a group vote at the **family meeting**. This makes them answerable to all the family members. It is also good if there is a younger sibling who has trouble asserting themselves.

ADD METHODS YOU HAVE USED:

_____
_____
_____

These are for children that are *unwilling* to cooperate in consequences.

451. Delay an outing for any time an item is delayed. Take care the penalty of this is only on the child. In other words make it an outing that is for the child, more than for the family.
452. Enlist the help of the family and have none of the members allow the child to borrow anything unless another family member is involved. Be sure to get a commitment of return time on paper then if the item is returned late, the next time the child wants to borrow something deny them that privilege.
453. Confiscate any borrowed item that comes in the house without permission and let the owner know when you return it that the child is not very responsible in that area and you would prefer if for the present they would not loan them things. Be sure as the child grows more responsible to contact these people and let them know. This not only builds self worth it allows the child the reward that goes with the behavior.
454. Build a chart and whenever the child borrows something write it down and bold face the return date. Any item not returned means no privileges happen until the item is returned.
455. Another way to do this if the child is saying things like "I don't have time," is a calendar in the child's room. You schedule or help schedule the day for the child and mark the items that need to be returned.
456. For items that are short term borrowed I find the best bet is if the child doesn't return it on time, without reminding, simply say "no" the next time and let the child know it was because they were not responsible the last time. Then try it again the next time the child wants to borrow something.

Loses Things

This is a behavior that as often as not the parents end up paying the price for, so to speak. I am always careful to look at the item as something I will probably be stuck to replace no matter who it belongs to. A school book may be the child's problem but only until the school calls me and insists I pay for it to get the child's report card. So I do a kind of across the board consequence, I don't care who it belongs to, this is what needs to happen. The only real exception to that is if the child bought the item themselves.

These are for children that are *willing* to cooperate in consequences.
457. Have the child physically retrace their steps through the day or last time they saw it. If it was not at home have them use the phone to retrace.
458. Have the child replace the item out of their allowance or by earning the money.
459. Have the child, with your help, build in a maintenance program. List where all items are kept and don't put them down anywhere but this. You need to have your child at a point of commitment for this to not be manipulated, so take care that you only use it if the child wants to stop losing things as much as you want them to stop losing things.
460. Sit down with the child and pray that God will show you where the lost item is. It works folks and I use it more than any other thing.
461. Have the child write ten times I will put name of item back in name of proper place next time I use it.
462. Have the child walk to the place where the item should have been and count the steps and time it took them. Have them tell you the steps and time they have spent searching. This helps your child realize you are trying to help them along with building in an awareness of the need for organizational skills.

These are for children that are *unwilling* to cooperate in consequences.

463. Ignore the behavior surrounding the loss and calmly insist that the child retrace their steps before they can have any other privilege.
464. Replay their behavior back. If they are completely unwilling, that night at snack time say their own words back to them only using their snack as the item lost. This will teach them that others are affected. Try to gain a willingness to search for the item or replace it.
465. Start withdrawing snacks or allowance money to replace the item. Assure the child this is the result of their unwillingness and is subject to change once they become willing.
466. Withdraw all similar items and put them on a check out basis. The child must come to you to get the item and must return it to you after they are finished. This is time consuming so only do it for a day or two. You can even cut it down to hours if you want. Again your goal is to get the child's cooperation.
467. Role model the right behavior. Call the child when you are putting things in their right place and reinforce you do this so you won't lose them. Do this whenever you think of it, the repetition helps the child remember and the time you take of the child's builds in the cost. Continue to try and get a commitment to work on the problem out of the child. Let them know once they are working on it you will stop the teaching.
468. Assert the positive. Whenever the child did not lose something let them know that you noticed and are proud of that behavior.

ADD METHODS YOU HAVE USED:

_____
_____
_____

Dresses Poorly

I speak here of the child who will not take the time or energy to clean and put on decent clothes. Some children are dressing what I consider poorly, but in their peer group it is acceptable. A good example is the style that demands jeans be ripped at the knees.

These are for children that are *willing* to cooperate in consequences.

469. Have the child do a dress code plan. Get ink and have them mark their outfits, dress and play. Once a week monitor the dress items to make sure they are in proper condition to wear for the following week.
470. Have the child set out clothes and accessories the night before. Monitor any changes before the child can go to bed.
471. Set in a deadline for having clothes ready. I like to use Saturday morning before they can go on any outings. All their clothes must be picked and ready for the coming week.
472. Set a goal with child. Plan the outfits they will wear during the week together. Offer a reward such as letting a boy use Dad's aftershave or a girl one of Mom's earnings for a complete follow through of the week. If the problem is severe make the goal easier to reach.
473. Have them read Dress for Success or other articles that teach the importance of correct dressing.
475. Challenge them to read magazines and try to match how the models in them look. You will need to help them see some of the things they have around that will match up to how they use them.

These are for children that are *unwilling* to cooperate in consequences.

476. You take over their choice of what they will wear the following day. Assure them they can try again tomorrow if they will have their clothes laid out the night before to show them to you.
478. Take over the washing and pressing of their clothes for the week, but also raise their bedtime to match the extra time they are adding to your schedule. Again assure them that this is not your first choice it is the choice their behavior is dictating.
479. Have a morning inspection. If the clothing is not appropriate have them change before you get them breakfast. Of course you delay breakfast not deny it.
480. Ignore the dress, but put in a reward system for every time they are dressed appropriate.
481. Be honest about your feelings on their appearance. Do not allow them to go with you unless they have taken the trouble to dress right. Don't forget taking them from school or to some place they wish to go is "with you."

ADD METHODS YOU HAVE USED:

_____
_____
_____
_____

Incomplete Chores

These are for children that are *willing* to cooperate in consequences.

482. Put in a penalty of one extra thing that needs to be done if the chore is not done properly. Explain that this makes up for the time you must spend monitoring.
483. Have the child build a chart listing all of the parts of the chore, then post it and have them check off each part as they complete it and bring the chart to you.
484. Have them redo the part they missed the first time. Remind them of it the next day right before they go to do the chore.
485. At a **family meeting** confront the behavior and have the child come up with consequences that they feel might help them remember.
486. Have them recite the adage "Any job worth doing is worth doing right" then tell you why they think that is important in life. Still have them go and do the job correctly.

These are for children that are *unwilling* to cooperate in consequences.

487. Ignore the behavior and do it yourself. When the child makes a request of you say sure after you do…I advise you make it something that takes more time and energy than finishing the chore you gave.
488. Take the chore away from them for a day to a week. Let them know the way they do it is showing you that they are not mature enough to handle it. At the same time take away some age given privilege. Examples of these are picking the show they want to watch, their bedtime, or choice of snack. Let them know that if they are not ready for the responsibility of that age group they are probably not ready for the privileges of it. Allow them a chance to earn it back.
489. Do the chore then be too tired to engage in some activity they want you to do. Explain that you can spend the time with them because of the help they give you.

ADD METHODS YOU HAVE USED:

_____
_____
_____
_____

Incomplete Schoolwork

Realize that the majority of this problem belongs to your child and your school. As a parent there is only so much that we can do and mostly, it is to set a standard on completion of tasks taken on. Schools vary in their willingness to help resolve the problem. I will say a parent that becomes a time consumer to a teacher will probably get more done than the parent who the teacher never sees.

These are for children that are *willing* to cooperate in consequences.

490. Meet with the teacher and set in a plan where all work not completed in class becomes homework. Have her send you a list home of the work uncompleted.
491. Break the work down into small components for the child. Work with them to teach them to do one small part of the work at a time.
492. Turn it into a group project. Have one member help the child each night to complete the day's work. Offer a family reward the first week *if* the schoolwork is all completed in school.
493. Set up school conferences weekly until the behavior has been corrected. Have the child present at these.
494. Have the child drop one of their other activities and utilize the time doing the work that has not been done in school.

These are for children that are *unwilling* to cooperate in consequences.

495. Ignore the wrong behavior. Build in some small reward for any day that the schoolwork is completed; perhaps their choice of a TV show after school. Try to connect the reward to the behavior. An example would be, doesn't it feel good to have your school work done, now you can watch whatever you would like today.
496. Pull in peer support. Ask the child's friends if they get their schoolwork done in class. When you find one who does, ask if they would be willing to come over for an hour twice a week and help your child. Monitor that time or it may end up just another play time.
497. Set up an after school tutor who will help the child do any uncompleted work that should have been done at school.
498. Take away one of the child's fun school activities and put that time aside for doing the unfinished work. The school will often work with you on this if the child has electives.
499. Ignore the behavior. Allow the child to accept the consequences that the school will put in; summer school, failing grades, or special classes. Make the child aware you will **not help them out and they will pay that price.**
500. If the problem is a disruption to class or very severe you can go to school with the child one or two days a week. With older children even the thought that I might do that gets a much more concentrated effort. If you don't have a day, then pick a time during school but only say what you can and will do.

ADD METHODS YOU HAVE USED:

_____
_____
_____
_____

Daydreaming

There is a certain amount of daydreaming that is part of growing up. I don't think it is harmful as much as it is sometimes annoying to parents. The problem is when daydreaming becomes an occupation, so to speak. It interferes with attention that needs to be given elsewhere. For that reason a fair amount of my consequences deal with grounding the child back in reality.

These are for children that are *willing* to cooperate in consequences.

501. Call their attention to it and the fact that it steals time from them. Ask them to tell you what they are thinking about. Bring that into what it would take to make it real and set a plan.
502. Set in some guidelines as far as when the child could spend daydreaming. Give them an hour a day when it does not interfere with any other activity.
503. Give the child a cue or phrase to help make them aware of when they do it. I like snapping their fingers because the noise seems to help them come back to the now. To paraphrase that each time you or the child find themselves daydreaming have the child snap their fingers.
504. Start morning mediation or reading; focus it on living in the here and now. This is probably the most effective one I have used because it starts the day keeping the child aware of their goal.
505. Have the child chart the time they spend daydreaming and what it costs them. Time and opportunities missed. Help them see what they are trading and the losses involved.

These are for children that are *unwilling* to cooperate in consequences.

506. Set in reality grounding. Every few hours check and say I am glad to see you so much into today. You really seem to have been staying busy and I like it.
507. Try to include in their life, activities that keep them busy and focused. If it can be things they enjoy so much the better. Some good examples are bowling, word games, activities that require their attention. Video games also require concentration. Try to teach them that they are concentrating on the present with these games so it is a skill they have.
508. Remove some of their TV or radio time. Channel that time into one of the above. Explain that you are concerned about their not seeming to be "with" you a large amount of the time.
509. Use a chart to monitor the time you must ask several times or you find the child in the chair drifting. By charting it you make the child face the reality of your concerns. The chart in itself forms the awareness so you really don't need a further consequence.
510. Role model the behavior you want. Pick times during the day to say, "I really have to pay attention to this or I might ____." Allow the child to name some danger to daydreaming.
511. I also like games that teach. Create a game where you share something that daydreaming cost you. Ask the child to do the same. You can mix it up by adding things you gained by being aware or add other behaviors. I try to give no opinion but allow the child an opportunity to count the cost.

ADD METHODS YOU HAVE USED:
_____
_____
_____

Wastes Food

These are for children that are *willing* to cooperate in consequences.

512. Start a self serving process. Allow the child to take their own portions, but only as long as they eat what they take. If they don't, you portion their food the next meal and try again.
513. Have the child make up a cost chart and price the wasted food. Come up with a weekly cost and when child lowers this loss, allow them to spend the amount on foods of their choice.
514. Set some goals for the child. You can have desert only if you eat your meal. Be sure to still keep the portions small.
515. If the problem is certain food, work on alternative choices in that food group; salad, in place of a cooked vegetable.
515. Make the child responsible for the wasted food. A good chore to let them earn the money is to plan the grocery shopping or meals the next week. They must supply all the food groups and consider the preparation time. Also give them a bottom line cost.

These are for children that are *unwilling* to cooperate in consequences.

516. Reduce the portions to extremely small. After the child eats that allow them more.
517. If it is certain items, serve them first, and allow the rest of the meal only after they have eaten the item. Make sure the amount of the item is very small. I find I am much more successful if I stress to the child that this system will stop as soon as they will give me some substitutes I can use.
518. Remove all snacks and deserts until the waste stops. Hunger makes food taste much better. Try to keep your time for doing this short because it is easy for this to move into a power struggle.
519. Make a point to make one of the child's favorites. Use the preferred food as the reward for the not wasted food.
520. Rather than meals, give small amounts of the meals throughout the day. Explain to the child you are trying to get the proper nutrition in them without the waste.

ADD METHODS YOU HAVE USED:

_____
_____
_____
_____

Doesn't Keep You Informed

The type of behavior I refer to here is not a deliberate avoidance. Those are far more like sneaking out. I find that children respond to an adjustment of those consequences. I refer here to a careless not considering of you.

These are for children that are *willing* to cooperate in consequences.
521. Have a family meeting and set in a mandatory three day notice of all activities. Without the notice they do not go.
522. Have the child do a weekly schedule of upcoming events and present it to you once a week. I like this because it also helps you budget your time.
523. Frame in their free time. You can have between 6:00 and 8:00 that is yours. "I need to know in advance what you plan to do with it". If they are late remove that amount of time from the beginning of the following day.
524. Form a pact with the child that you will both keep each other informed of the upcoming activities. Make a reward that each can do for the other if you have a perfect week.
525. Agree that each time the child is out without telling you where, they will list at least five things that they could have done to let you know.

These are for children that are *unwilling* to cooperate in consequences.

526. Delay the next place they want to go explaining to them that they need to keep you informed.
527. Call around. Whenever they are not where they need to be, start making calls to their friends and people they know. This probably makes for a better deterrent than anything else because the child can see the ripple affect.
528. Refuse to take the child the next time until they put in writing where they want to go and the time they will return. If they have informed you, tell them they don't have to write it and stress why.
529. Role model the behavior. Keep informing the child of your plans and let them know it is also what you expect from them.
530. Withhold an outing. Simply refuse to take them because you were not told in advance.
531. Call where the child is going and let the parent know when they are expected back. Do this in front of the child explaining they have shown you that you cannot trust them to return on time.

ADD METHODS YOU HAVE USED:

_____
_____
_____
_____

Bed Wetting

Do not overlook the obvious on this. If a child is asleep then in many ways they are not in control. Although the behavior is quite discomforting to the parents, it is also hard for the child.

* Note: **Consult a physician** to rule out a medical problem *first*.

These are for children that are *willing* to cooperate in consequences.
532. Have the child clean the linens themselves. Allow them to get up early so that they will have time to do this.
533. Give the child an alarm clock and set it for an hour or two after they fall asleep. Have them get up and use the bathroom.
534. Work with the child on the amount of liquids they take in at night. Try to stop all liquid intake about three hours before bed. Or better yet work as a team to find out how soon you must stop liquids to stop bed wetting.
535. Have the child go to bed a little later and rise a little earlier. Get them into the habit of going to the bathroom directly before they fall asleep.

These are for children that are *unwilling* to cooperate in consequences.

536. Take them to the doctor and check that there is not some internal reason for the problem. Have the doctor talk with child on some choices they can make.
537. Stop all liquids from dinner onward. If necessary store them in your room and make the kitchen off limits. Try to get the child to be willing to cooperate with you by saying you would be more flexible if they would help you chart times that work.
538. Wash their linens, but take the time from some other outing you would normally take them on. Again give them the choice of doing their linen.
539. Set in a reward system for every night the child does not wet the bed. Try to connect the reward to the behavior. Such as "you didn't drink and wet the bed last night. I think you deserve to stay up a little later so you can go to the bathroom a little later."
540. Wake the child up an hour after they are asleep and take them to the bathroom. This one makes you pay the price so realize you'll have to be consistent if you want it to work. Ask yourself if you are willing to do that.

ADD METHODS YOU HAVE USED:

_____
_____
_____
_____

Skipping School

These are for children that are *willing* to cooperate in consequences.

541. Sort through the behavior with the child and find out the reason. Then set in a consequence that solves the problem. An example would be a hard test is the reason, the consequence might be a study time.
542. If the behavior is based on activities they could not otherwise do, set in a schedule to do those things if at all possible. If not, come up with, and make sure they do the other things they have chosen. Make sure the child pays the school consequence for skipping.
543. Hold a school meeting and decide with teachers some way that the child can redo all the work that is done. The child will not get credit for it but it will make it a no gain situation.
544. You gather all the work and use a weekend day for make-up time. Be sure the hours included are the same and that the work load includes phys-ed if the child has it.
545. Give child extra homework time throughout the week. Make the hours equal up to the time they skipped.

These are for children that are *unwilling* to cooperate in consequences.

546. Ignore the behavior but be sure to check with school to find out if the child has paid whatever consequence the school enforces.
548. Start calling the school during the daytime to make sure the child is there. If they are not, call and report it to the local authorities. Make sure your child is aware of your plan of action.
549. Refuse to help in all trust based activities until trust is earned back. If child wants you to take them to a friend's say, "No, you lost my trust when you skipped school and now it will take a while to earn it back." Remember that the goal is to have the child succeed, so either set it on a time limit, or say, "You earned some trust by going to school today so I will take you."
550. Take the child for a visit of a more controlled school setting. You can ask your guidance counselor if the child can spend one or two periods in the class. If that is not possible ask one of your local mental health facilities if they will let you tour one of their treatment classrooms. Point out to the child the probability they will be in one of these classes if the behavior continues.

ADD METHODS YOU HAVE USED:

_____
_____
_____
_____

Overuses Products

This is a behavior that is hard for me because, how much is enough? The secondary issue is always, "I didn't do it". These are both best addressed at a **family meeting** and if necessary the consequences set in for the whole family.

These are for children that are *willing* to cooperate in consequences.

551. If the product is family used; toilet paper, laundry soap, catsup, put in family guidelines on how much a month is spent on the item. If over that amount is used let each member pitch in an equal amount of money to purchase another bottle.
552. Start to monitor the amounts and put small amounts out. If you see the child using too much, only allow half of what they need the next two times. Explaining you must replace the amount gone.
553. Set in practice sessions where you monitor the use of the product. Make sure you can follow through on this one. I find it best to say you can only do laundry Saturday morning so that I can see how much detergent you are using.
554. If the product is personal; shampoo, deodorant, or such, let the child know how much you will be buying and do not buy any more. If they run out, they will have to buy their own or substitute with another item.
555. Teach the correct amounts to the child. Set a time aside to go over how much they are using and how much they should be using. Measure the amounts out to get a clear picture.

These are for children that are *unwilling* to cooperate in consequences.

556. Give the child a cash amount to cover the supplies they need. Be sure not to rescue the child if they run out. Keep a helpful but firm attitude.
557. For family items insist in monitoring their use and hide the product. Be careful if the item is chore related not to do the work, simply the applying of the article. In other words don't do their laundry, simply put in the detergent. Make this an "earn back the responsibilities by proper use" so you don't get caught doing it for life.
558. Exchange the product you normally buy for less expensive ones. Be sure the child is aware that the problem is the amount being used and that the family can go back to the better product if usage drops.
559. When you buy the product, put a replacement date on it. Let the child know that is the date you will be replacing it so the choice of how to make it last, is theirs.
560. Build in a reward. When you give them the product explain if they can make it last a long time that you will be able to afford a better product next time.

ADD METHODS YOU HAVE USED:

_____
_____
_____
_____

Doesn't Clean Room

Probably the **number one** problem parents have and certainly a place where children assert their independence.

These are for children that are *willing* to cooperate in consequences.
561. Hold a **family meeting** and define clean, come to an agreement of how often various things need to be done. Make a chart that can be checked off and allow a snack after the child shows you the chart.
562. Wake the child ½ hour earlier if the room is not cleaned one day in order to allow extra time in the morning to clean it.
563. Do not allow any privileges until after the room is cleaned.
564. Form a team effort and give special recognition to the most responsible person of the week. The one who kept their room the most consistently clean.
565. Break the job into pieces and put a time frame and reward on each part. "Make your bed then you can have breakfast. Clothes picked up before you can go play." This is very successful with kids who get overwhelmed easily.

These are for children that are *unwilling* to cooperate in consequences.

566. Clean the room yourself and take a monitory amount for your services from their allowance. Make sure the cash amount does not go over what you would pay them for the chore.
567. Do not make an issue at the time. When a weekend or some other occasion comes where the child needs your help, explain you will be glad to help *after* the room is clean. Stress their unwillingness has created the inconvenience.
568. Remove most of the extra articles from the room explaining that they can be earned back by showing that the child can care for them. That means keeping the place where they are, clean.
569. Set in a small consequence such as "Nothing new can go into your room while it is dirty," then ignore the behavior, but give small verbal and privilege rewards when the room is clean. Make a big deal out of the fact the child cleaned it.
570. Don't worry about it and make one day a week a clean up day either by the child or by you. If you have to do it, set up the room so it is easy to clean and explain that it is necessary because they are not acting responsibility. Have the child stay in the room while you clean it. Try to teach the child while you are there about the losses and gains of being responsible.

ADD METHODS YOU HAVE USED:
_____
_____
_____
_____

Set up Behaviors

These are the purer than pure behaviors that make a parent doubt their own sanity. If I were to color them they would probably be in shades of white; somewhat like dirty snow to the color of slush; the overlooking of a sibling, depending on them to wake them up, as a few footprints dirtying the snow. The constant belittlement of others, and you being the slush, that chills you all the way to the bone. The reason is fairly simple. The desire of this child's heart is to be **perfect**, or at least more perfect than anyone else around them. They cannot allow themselves to look bad, so someone else must take the blame.

I think the basic emotion behind the behavior is a need to feel *worthy* and have a right to exist. As the yellows of carelessness find their roots in self worth so do the whites of "set up behavior". It is my own feeling that the major difference is in the child believing they cannot be wrong. They overly fear the judgment of others or the judgment they impose on themselves. We are often our own worst critics.

Because the answer lays in the realization that perfection is a goal, that mistakes are things to learn and grow by, much of what has to occur is seeing a broader picture of the world. Feeling the results of misbehavior is not so important.

I choose to keep the focus on consequences that teach rather than that make the child responsible. I guess I have found that if these kids realize mercy also has its place, they and we as parents will be far better off.

I also have found this type of child to be extremely competitive. They seem to spend their life looking at an imaginary score card that rates them to others. By setting others up, they give themselves points. One thing experience has taught me NEVER use the information this child gives you to make a judgment on another. That seems to work in about the same manner as pouring gas on a smoldering fire. It really escalates the behavior. It is challenging to evaluate my own actions in this area also. Do I act like "He who makes the least mistakes is the one who has the right to exist"? For myself, I must say there have been times. If my family starts to use words like self righteous to describe me, I am off track again.

Tips to remember:
1. Set-up work has its roots in perfectionism.
2. Any behavior that seems punishing furthers this erroneous view.
3. It is truly a desire to be a good person.
4. The child confuses being good with being worthwhile.
5. Looking at my messages in worthiness of people helps.
6. These kids keep a scoreboard in their heads.

Loud Music

Children generally like their music louder than adults. The behavior I speak of here is the child that seems to pick their time and bait someone into hollering at them.

These are for children that are *willing* to cooperate in consequences.
570. Ask why they find it necessary to annoy you. Wait for a response. If the child defends it simply restate they are being annoying and that they need to turn the radio down.
571. Point out that they are annoying others and people are more important than things so if you hear it up again you will have to take it for a half hour. If it goes up again take it.
572. Set in boundaries allowing for loud music at certain times such as 6:00 P.M. to 8:00 P.M. Then, when the music goes on instead of saying no you can say *wait*. This will build in cooperation and also help the child look at their motives and goals.
573. Build in a more confronting way to act. Explain that you feel they are doing it to annoy and say "When the music goes up I will come in, turn it off, and spend ten minutes trying to figure out what is going on inside you."
574. Create a chart noting the times of loud music and explore other options at your **family meeting**. Such as after school I will take a walk with a walkman before I come in my room and then I won't be so tempted to turn it up.
575. Have them buy earphones. This allows the child freedom to block out problems, yet stops the set-up work.

These are for children that are *unwilling* to cooperate in consequences.

576. Put a mark on the radio's volume knob where it is not allowed to be above. If you find it above the mark, set the knob and take the knob off for a day or two.
577. Take the radio for five minutes each time it is above the agreed upon level. I find if I don't mark the level there is resistance over how high *it really was*. If you get that response, allow them only to listen to it after **you** set the markings and are there to see they don't change them.
578. If the problem happens when you have company what I like to do is excuse myself and go trip the fuse box. This forces the child to confront me in public and makes them unsure if I am the cause. I usually say that I guess the music was loud enough to blow the fuse. It has the impact of a well-planned party trick and rarely embarrasses guests. Don't fix the fuse for at least five minutes.
579. Make the radio disappear. Do not confront the issue at the time. The next time the child is gone simply take the radio and refuse to return it until the child will sit down with you and come up with a plan of action that meets everyone's needs.
580. Ignore the behavior and when you are together refuse to allow the radio in the car. Simply explain that you hear enough of their music already because of the volume they put it at.

ADD METHODS YOU HAVE USED:

_____
_____
_____
_____

Interrupting

These are for children that are *willing* to cooperate in consequences.

581. Have the child write five times, "It is rude to interrupt." and make sure they leave the room to do it.
582. Give the child a choice to stay in the same room and not interrupt or to leave the room until you are finished talking to the other person. If they interrupt again they are telling you by their actions that they wish to leave.
583. Cut off the child by saying "When you do that I feel hurt, but you can make it up to me by bringing me coffee." The exact wording doesn't matter as long as it confronts the problem and forces the child to do something therefore stopping what they were going to say.
584. At a **family meeting** set in a penalty for interrupting that the whole family must follow. I find this very good for helping me stay aware when I interrupt. Make it something small like being quiet for the next two minutes.
585. Let the child finish what they were going to say then let them know you expect them to be quiet for the same period of time since they took their conversation time already.

These are for children that are *unwilling* to cooperate in consequences.

586. Excuse yourself. You and the person who you are talking to go into another room away from the child. Note: *the child may use another means to distract you.*
587. Stop all conversation even after the child is done and explain that you are waiting for them to get all of the talking out of their system. The silence will act as a tool and the child will probably get angry and leave. After you are done talking, be sure to go to the child and let them know why you reacted as you did and how they can prevent it happening again. The trick to this is in not responding to the child at all.
588. Pre-teach. If you do not want to be interrupted let the child know in advance that you expect them to not interrupt while you are talking to so and so. If possible give them the choice to color or write what they want to say.
589. Be direct. Immediately stop the child and say in a calm, but firm voice, "You interrupted. That was rude and I don't like it so please wait until _____ is finished." Be sure to ask the child if they wait, what they wanted to say.
590. Ignore the behavior. Just let the child finish, but don't respond to them. Apologize to the person for the child and act as if the incident is done. If the child confronts you as in "Mom I need____." Tell the child you have no intention of responding while they are interrupting, but give them a time you will discuss it later.

ADD METHODS YOU HAVE USED:

_____
_____
_____
_____

Constant Chattering

This is one I notice parents dealing with at **stores**. I enjoy watching people and I can see mom's particularly worn to the bone with trying to keep up with this. Feeling the need never to ignore what their child has to say. I must stress that your child does need to learn and have time to share with you, but that is not incessant chattering about nothing.

These are for children that are *willing* to cooperate in consequences.
591. Address the problem directly. Explain that the constant noise is wearing on you and try for two minutes of silence to use the other senses.
592. Use a diversionary tactic. Tell child that you want them to look for something or do something for you. If you are in a car turn it into a game. We will be quiet for three minutes then share all the sounds or sights that we experienced.
593. Talk to the child and teach them to think about what they are going to say. You can do that by mirroring their words back to them and asking why they wanted to tell you that or if they just wanted to talk?
594. Have the child who is chattering count to ten before they speak. I only use this for a short time and mostly with kids who talk to cover nervousness. It does help them learn, but it can also be annoying to the child and seem senseless.
595. Have a plan. Sit with the child and plan talk times and times that it is wise to be quiet. Help the child figure out some things they can do during quiet times. I like games like pretend you are a mute what must that feel like? With that you also can teach the child empathy for others.

These are for children that are *unwilling* to cooperate in consequences.

596. Hold a **family meeting** and address the problem. Have the other family members share their perception of what the child does and what might help the child stop. Try to set in guidelines for how much talking is enough and what talk is important to you.
597. Pre-teach. If the behavior occurs in stores or when out, sit with the child beforehand and tell them you want them to be quiet during certain times. Be specific for both of your sakes. If they do not observe those limits inform them you will go home that much earlier. Make sure you take a slot of the time that is pleasant for the child.
598. Build in a slot of time just for talking, "We will go to the park and spend fifteen minutes talking if I get this amount of silence during our outing." You can also do this at home by just putting in a sharing time.
599. State the truth, as in, "I need some quiet," then just walk away. Keep going back to the problem of the chattering. Be sure to build in the desired goals and be specific in time frames because kids don't have a clear idea of how much talk is too much talk.

ADD METHODS YOU HAVE USED:
_____
_____
_____
_____

Shows Off

I need to be clear here. It is normal and good for children to share their successes. I speak of children who do it in an inappropriate manner that puts down others, or puts them at risk.

These are for children that are *willing* to cooperate in consequences.
600. Have the child rephrase the sentence so it does not put down another. "I climb that tree better than Johnny," could be restated to "I like climbing trees and I feel good about that."
601. Have the child give two other ways that they could have said or done something that would not have made them look like a show off.
602. If it is a center stage behavior like asking anyone who comes in the house to watch them perform, set in a time for the child to share with company and go over the type of things that will not be offensive. Remind the child if they begin to perform.
603. Give the child an outlet for their talents. If it is singing, get them in choir, sports, get them on a little league team. Have them agree to only using the talent at that time.
604. If it is a dangerous, impulsive, type behavior, as in watch me climb to the top of the tree or look at me riding the bike down the highway with no hands; set in some firm limits. Have the child tell you why that is not wise and four other things they would not be wise to try. This consequence teaches limits for new behaviors and allows a child to think it out—so I like it.

These are for children that are *unwilling* to cooperate in consequences.

605. Hold a **family meeting** and have everyone share how the show off behavior makes them feel. Decide as a unit if the behavior starts, that the family will ignore it.
606. Ignore the behavior. Give positive attention every time you see the child act as a part of the group, or not center stage. This is easy to do because rarely does someone spend all their time showing off. It is hard to remember because rarely do we praise our kids for doing *nothing*.
607. If it is verbal "I am better than," give the attention to the other party. "I dress so much nicer than Susie." You could answer with "Susie probably doesn't have the style sense you do, but she is warm and caring, perhaps I could help her with that." You moved the focus over to the person they want to feel better than and defeated their goal.
608. Give the child a short adage or a spiritual message in response to the behavior. "Pride goeth before a fall, so I'd be careful."
609. If it is dangerous actions take away the possibility of doing it for a short time, but allow the child to earn it back by telling you why it was dangerous and four other things it would not be wise to do. An example would be "Now, you cannot ride your bike for five minutes or you can tell me why that was not a smart thing to do."

ADD METHODS YOU HAVE USED:

_____
_____
_____
_____

Blames Others

This is a behavior that drives me nuts! No matter what has happened, it is because Susie talked them into it, or Johnny said it would be OK, or Joey's family does it. These are not consequences for the misbehavior, so don't reward the misbehavior by letting the child off the hook to set these consequences in. What I will often do is give the child time to cool down and get these done, then bring up the behavior again.

These are for children that are *willing* to cooperate in consequences.
610. Hold a **family meeting** and set in a guideline that all behavior belongs to the person who did it. Anyone blaming another owes the other person an apology for attempting to set them up.
611. Have the child tell you five people who did *not* engage in the behavior.
612. Have the child tell you five people who they consider leaders, then ask them how they feel those people would have reacted in the same circumstances.
613. Very gently say "Shh, I want you to do your consequence first and think about what you are going to tell me. If you still want to tell me after that, then you can." If the child tells you later just say "oh", or "really." Something short that gives it no power and then *change the subject*.
614. Have the child identify what they are doing. Have them tell you how they think they would feel if they were the other person.

These are for children that are *unwilling* to cooperate in consequences.

615. Confront the person being blamed and ask if they are aware that the child is trying to hold them responsible for this behavior. Ask the other person how they feel about that. Make sure your child **is present** when you do this.
616. You state five different people who might have not participated in the behavior. If the child refuses to listen to you, do not push the issue, but when the child wants to speak to you, come back to the subject.
617. Ignore the behavior entirely and focus on what was done. Next time you make a mistake smile and look at the child and say, "It was____." (Whoever he blamed), the last time fault. Then attempt to talk about how unrealistic it is to blame others for your actions.
618. Excuse yourself for a few minutes and come back saying you'll discuss this matter only as long as the words the child uses remain in (I, me, myself). This works well if the child wants attention, but can be used against you if your child uses diversion to draw you away from the problem. The trick is not to let the original behavior get lost.

ADD METHODS YOU HAVE USED:

_____
_____
_____
_____

Minimizing

I am referring here to the child who acts as if the behavior had no importance at all and you are being totally unjust in even considering it as a problem.

These are for children that are *willing* to cooperate in consequences.

619. Have the child call a local specialist and get their reaction to the problem. Don't forget that this is *not* the consequence for the behavior but *for minimizing* it.
620. Sit with the child and form solid and clear boundaries. Write them somewhere so you are sure that you both know what you consider misbehavior. If you have that already in existence show it to them.
621. Have the child discover the reasons themselves by asking for a report or a research paper on the particular behavior. You may want to limit the sources as some children might misuse this.
622. Use spiritual literature to teach the importance of following rules. Also teach that there is a way to get rules changed and it is not arguing with the enforcer. Have the child bring it up in the **family meeting**.

These are for children that are *unwilling* to cooperate in consequences.

623. State clearly that you do not want to debate and that the child is welcome to bring it to the **family meeting** if they disagree. Either change the subject yourself, or walk away from the child if they continue.
624. Allow the child to vent, sit calmly until they are through. Say something like, "Good points," or "Oh." Then say again, "This is the consequence for this behavior."
625. Tell the child you will be glad to listen, but only after they have done the consequence for the behavior.
626. If the behavior is one that is deemed wrong by society, i.e.; stealing, lying, riding a bike without a helmet. Offer to help the child write a letter to the proper official, but only after they have completed the consequence.

ADD METHODS YOU HAVE USED:

_____
_____
_____
_____

Belittles

These are for children that are *willing* to cooperate in consequences.

627. Put in a family *rule* that any negative comment requires *four positives*. That means that if someone says, "You're dumb," they must follow that with, "Your pretty, kind, helpful, and understanding." (These must be *real* compliments).
628. Have the child take the negative comment and see the positive personality parts in it. Johnny is a liar, this also means he knows right from wrong, is teachable because he doesn't want to get in trouble, doesn't like people angry at him, wants our approval. Then have the child see ways he might help the person gain these skills.
629. Very simply ask the child what they are doing and why are they doing it. Don't accept an answer like, "Because he is." Come back to why is it so important for them to tell you that. Lead the child to a deeper understanding of themselves. Does it make them feel better than another, or do they expect you will fix the problem. Will you see them as a helpless victim? What do they hope to gain?
630. Bring the focus back to the child. Yes, Johnny does do that sometimes, can you think of a time you have ever done that? Lessen the behavior if you need to, and help the child identify with it. Ask them what made them do that. Then go back to Johnny and ask if the motives could be the same.

These are for children that are *unwilling* to cooperate in consequences.

631. Cut the child off when they start and say, "That behavior makes me want to defend the other person and think less of you, so I want no part of it."
632. Hear the child out then simply say, "So?" Give it little or no attention. Choose a later time to talk about the good you see in the person being belittled.
633. Move the focus back to the child by saying, "Now tell me what is wrong with *you* since we all have things we can work on in ourselves." Those are the only real important things, the ones you can change in yourself.
634. Leave. State that is not something you care to hear and leave the room.
635. At the **family meeting** bring it up and allow all other members of the family to share how it makes them feel and what their probable reaction to it is.

ADD METHODS YOU HAVE USED:

_____
_____
_____
_____

Hiding Things

This refers to a subtle revenge method of some children. It is a way of gaining control of others and not carelessness. I would advise parents to trust their gut on this and if it feels deliberate then it probably is.

These are for children that are *willing* to cooperate in consequences.
636. Put in a rule that any person caught with another person's things becomes responsible to pay for them. This will not stop the hiding but will give you some control over who is touching what.
637. You and the child look for the item. Stop all other activities until it is found. This makes for inconvenience; your child's as well yours.
638. Sit the child down and be honest. Say you suspect that they hid the article. Have them go into their room and think about it, while you look. After you find it, go over again with the child your suspicions. Bring it up a third time at dinner.
639. Enlist the child's help. Say. "I know I put my earrings here and now they are gone. Pray with me that we locate them. I want to look in the bedroom; where do you want to look?"

1001 NATURAL LOGICAL CONSEQUENCES

These are for children that are *unwilling* to cooperate in consequences.

640. Make an issue about it. A large percentage of this behavior being successful lies in the fact that the child makes you doubt your own sanity. Do not bend on the fact that you *know* it was moved.
641. If at all possible make it a dual ownership problem. "My purse is missing. I left it here and now it is gone. Snack will be late because I must look for it, so you will have to either wait on your snack or help me look."
642. Keep a close surveillance on the child. Be honest about the fact that you do not trust them and why. Try to keep the items that are important to you in an off limits room.
643. Don't give it any attention at all. Look for the item away from the child, show no annoyance. If the goal of the child is to upset you this will defeat the goal and you may be surprised at how well it works.

ADD METHODS YOU HAVE USED:

_____
_____
_____
_____

Tattles

Bear in mind that as a parent you are like the police. Your job is to enforce the rules. Your child's job is to come to the authority figure when the rules are being broken. That is not tattling. I find the best guideline for me is this. Is the child telling me to protect themselves or to hurt or control the other person?

These are for children that are *willing* to cooperate in consequences.

644. Sit the child down and explain that the telling on others separates them from the other children. It also makes you think less of them. A more positive answer is to take a stand with the person on whatever the issue is. Send them back to resolve the issue.
645. Sit down with both parties and act as a mediator. The trick here is to say as little as possible. An example would be "We called you here because Jill has some concerns, Jill will you share them with her?" After the child has expressed them say, "Helen, what do you have to say?" Your goal is to get the offender to decide to make it right, and the tattler to see the power that they have to settle the problem. Avoid becoming the enforcer or you *reward* the negative behavior of tattling.
646. Make a contract with the child that agrees to come to you for advice on how to handle minor situations, but the handling of them is up to the child. Set a time limit on how long you will spend with them or it may become as difficult to handle as the tattling.
647. Work together to build in some concrete goals for problem managing. If Tommy gets dirty it is not something to run to me with. If he has a knife and is threatening you and others with it, it is. Be sure to add some concrete solutions that the child can use for Tommy's getting dirty.
648. Set in a small reward for the times that the child manages to handle a problem without tattling. I like to set a special time aside to go over them and give lots of encouragement for this.

These are for children that are *unwilling* to cooperate in consequences.

649. Don't give the tattling any power. Don't set in consequences on the offender if at all possible. Sit and talk with the other person and try very hard to get the person to decide to do the right thing. Stress that they were not *caught* doing anything so you are there only as a concerned party.
650. If you need to set in a consequence because of the nature of the action, lessen it, explaining that you realize it came to you from another source and because of that you are being lenient. Stay aware that giving the tattler power over the other will only act against you and the tattler in the long run.
651. Simply say, "So?" then move the conversation back to the tattler by saying something like "My real concern here is why you find it necessary to bring every little thing that ___ does to me. Are you trying to be better than him?"
652. Ignore the behavior completely; giving some small response like, "I am sure ___ can handle that without my help." Then build in rewards every time you see the child handling their own problems. Move the focus to the positive and let them know you appreciate that.

ADD METHODS YOU HAVE USED:

_____
_____
_____
_____

Talks down about You to Others

In clarifying this behavior I must say that children need to express themselves and share their problems. If the slant on it is to hurt you or get you to change a behavior for their benefit, then you have a problem. Another poor reason for this is to try and let others see them in a victim role.

These are for children that are *willing* to cooperate in consequences.

653. Address the behavior, tell them it hurts you and ask them why they feel the need to do that. Make a pact that they will come to you if they have a problem rather than others.
654. Have a **family meeting** and put in a rule that four positives must be said before a negative. Then have the child share four positive things about you when they share one negative.
655. Have the child tell you the things that they feel are correct about you, explaining that they have now hurt you and it is their job to help heal you.
656. If the statements are untrue, have the child write you a letter of apology. Also show it to the other person and let them know that the child is working on this behavior.
657. Have the child tell you four other people who they could have shared this with and not had it create trouble. This might include a minister, friend, or teacher. Another slant on that is to have the child tell you a way they might have worded it to not cause trouble, this works well for the perpetual victim.

These are for children that are *unwilling* to cooperate in consequences.

658. At your **family meeting** address the issue and have the other family members share their feelings when someone talks poorly about them to others. Put in a *rule* that the family will try to *build up* any member who is being put down.
659. Make a reward box with tiny candies. One set of life savers and another set a strong bitter taste such as cloves or menthalyptus. Give the lifesavers for sweet words and the other for bitter words.
660. Go to the other person in front of the child and share that you are aware of what the child is saying. Tell the person what is going on, then ask how they think they might handle the same situation. Most people will be supportive of you.
661. Ignore the behavior entirely. This may be difficult, but the truth is that once it no longer gains any response, it will probably disappear. Reward all positive statements that the child makes to others about you.

ADD METHODS YOU HAVE USED:
_____
_____
_____
_____

Fakes Sickness

Remember there is a goal behind this. A problem the child doesn't feel they can handle, attention they feel they must have, or the need to control the parent's time. **Get to the goal** and you will correct the behavior.

These are for children that are *willing* to cooperate in consequences.

662. Sit with the child and set in guidelines for sick. Things like a fever, diarrhea, flushed skin. Explain that although the fake things may not feel particularly pleasant they will go away if you ignore them. They do not warrant medical care.
663. Put the child in control of their own health issues. Get a medical book and when the child complains have them look up the symptoms and make a diagnosis. Try to go with some old home remedies.
664. Make a pact with the child that they will go ahead and try to go to school or the activity and if they still feel the same way in two hours you will come and get them. Many times just the getting going distracts them.
665. Have a *rule* in the family that if anyone is too sick to fulfill their responsibilities then they are too sick to be out of bed until the next day. Do not let them be up and playing. You can act in a most nurturing manner, but let them know you don't want the strain on their eyes of TV or anything to stop their body from healing.
666. Have the child join you in praying for healing or health. Next, have the child spend at least an hour focusing their attention on other things. Another twist on that is to have the child call a minister or healing line.
667. Put the responsibility back on the child. Ask questions like "What do you think I should do?" or, "What do you think might make you feel better?"

These are for children that are *unwilling* to cooperate in consequences.

668. Put your focus on the cost of sickness to the child. Missed opportunities, lack of activities, the social or spiritual concept that they are not complete. Let them know you don't wish this for them and you believe they deserve more.
669. Use the old "Mom's home remedy kit." Give them chicken soup, or club soda. Any one of a variety of things that are convenient and say, "I care," without much change in your schedule or giving the child much power.
670. Ignore the behavior; in the sense that you give it very little attention. Simply do an, "Oh well". You will need to be careful on this because if you come across as indifferent you may get more of the behavior rather than less of it.
671. Take the child to the Doctor but rather than stressing that the child was wrong, stress the goodness of God for allowing the child health (assuming the good doctor says they are fine). Often the child forgets that health is a blessing.

ADD METHODS YOU HAVE USED:

_____
_____
_____
_____

Gets in the Way of Others

Here, I am speaking of children who place their body in a position to block another from doing what they want or need to do. This can range from sprawling across the floor so one cannot walk by to physically blocking a doorway you need to enter.

These are for children that are *willing* to cooperate in consequences.

672. Make the child aware of the problem and have them state other positions that they could have used that would not have annoyed others.
673. Have the child ask permission for the rest of the day to sit, stand, etc. This helps the child become more aware of their positioning.
674. Have the child tell you where they are going to place themselves and why, for the remainder of the day.
675. Set certain trouble areas as boxed in for the day. An example would be the child is sprawled across the floor watching TV and no one can get through. You say, "Jimmy you seem to be in everyone's way, so for the rest of today if you are in the recreation room, you need to be sitting in the blue chair."
676. Have the child make a list of the places where he has never gotten in trouble for being and post them on his wall as his goal.

These are for children that are *unwilling* to cooperate in consequences.

677. Hold a **family meeting** and have the family confront the child on the behavior and how it makes the other parties feel.
678. Withhold a privilege related to the space the child invaded. For example, "Tom I am taking the children to the movies. I cannot let you go because in the television room last night you were in the way and that shows me you cannot be responsible when you are watching a movie."
679. Reward the child whose space was invaded. If Andy was the injured party, explain that you know this is annoying and what you can do to make it better for him. Give the offender as little time and attention as possible for the behavior.
680. Preplan the seating or activities and do not let the offending party know till the end. Give the favored seats to those who do not engage in the behavior. Make the offender aware that they created this by their refusal to cooperate in a consequence.

ADD METHODS YOU HAVE USED:
_____
_____
_____
_____

Pouting

These are for children that are *willing* to cooperate in consequences.

681. Call the behavior to the child's attention, and come up with a more positive way to handle the behavior. Such as saying that what is going on makes them unhappy, writing a note, or walking away.
682. Have the child go into their room or out of sight until they can have a more positive expression.
683. Let the child know you can see they are upset by what is going on in their life. Have the child tell you seven things that are going right.
684. Have the child write you a note about what is going on. After you get it, fold it up and put it away for tomorrow. The next day look at it together and see how important the issue looks. Make the child aware that they are choosing to spend time they could otherwise spend having fun, with pouting.
685. When their expression is sour, have them take a spoon of sugar or sing a sweet song. Both actions divert the child and will give them the feeling of doing something with their unhappiness.
686. Offer to pray with the child that God will either change your heart or theirs because it hurts you to see them so unhappy.

These are for children that are *unwilling* to cooperate in consequences.

687. Smile at the child and let them know you can sense how they feel, but you don't feel bad because of what is going on. You are proud they can show that much control over their actions.
688. Ignore the behavior. Simply go on with your own affairs. When the child is more positive let them know you are glad they are feeling better.
689. You leave the room for a few minutes and return when the child's expression is less sour. If the child holds the pout for a while, simply leave again.
690. Point out the child's choices to them. They can pout, play a game with you, or go outside.
691. You can offer a small reward for stopping the pout. A good positive way to do that would be, "I am going to take a walk. I would love to have you join me if you were in a more pleasant mood." This gives the child the choice, but makes it in their best interest to stop pouting.

ADD METHODS YOU HAVE USED:
_____
_____
_____
_____

Spends Too Much Time at Friends

I refer here of an ongoing problem not of carelessness as addressed earlier. Rather a deliberate misstating or indifference to the time limits that have been set.

These are for children that are *willing* to cooperate in consequences.
692. Bring the problem to the **family meeting**. State the issues and the breaking of trust. Have the family come up with some consequences that might work. Also have the child come up with some consequences.
693. Have the child pay you back the time that was taken from you by doing enough for you to equalize the time that was spent.
694. If the child offers excuses such as there was no phone or no ride back. Have the child preplan the next outing complete with emergency plans. If the child cannot do that they cannot go.
695. Address the behavior and give the child a choice. Either they can choose to co-operate in one of the above behaviors or the next time they need a ride to a friends etc. you will tell them "no".

These are for children that are *unwilling* to cooperate in consequences.

696. Ignore the behavior other then telling them it is unfair to make you worry as they have been doing. The next time they go to a friend's, make a point of calling at least twice to remind them of the time they are to be home. Assure them you will trust them and stop calling when they become prompt.
697. When they ask to go somewhere call the parent or person in charge and make the plans for the time they are to be home. I like to do this in front of the child and again build in cues that they need to gain trust by cooperation.
698. Work with the child's friends. When whoever was with the child comes over, pull them off to the side and explain your feelings when your child is late. Ask what the other child can do to help assure that it won't happen again.
699. If the child wanders off alone and doesn't return on time try not letting them go alone for a while. Assure them that that privilege can be gained back by showing you promptness.

ADD METHODS YOU HAVE USED:

_____
_____
_____
_____

Making Faces

These are for children that are *willing* to cooperate in consequences.

700. Have them go into the bathroom immediately and make the face in the mirror. When they come out ask them how they think they looked. If they give you a feeling; angry, hurt, etc, it makes the perfect time to tell them other ways to express their feelings.
701. Ask the child why they found it necessary to make that face. Have them give you three more appropriate ways that might have gotten their needs met better.
702. Teach non-verbal cues. Have the child play a game with you like charades where everything is expressed non-verbally. Point out that much of what people "hear" them saying is not verbal. Have the child decide what messages they wish to give others.
703. If the problem is an on going one set in a face making time each day. Ten minutes where they can make all the faces they want. If the child goes to make a face remind them it is not time for that yet. Also, at the time make sure they make the face they tried to make earlier.

These are for children that are *unwilling* to cooperate in consequences.

704. Repeat the face expression back at them. Smile and keep your voice tone friendly. Ask the child "How do I look when I do that, do you think there might be some better ways I could let you know how I feel?" The key to this is **DO NOT COME ACROSS CYNICAL**. If the child picks that up, you will get more of the same from them.
705. Ignore the behavior completely. This is one behavior that if it gets no results, will eventually disappear. If it doesn't, make sure that they are not receiving some gain from a peer or other family member.
706. Address the behavior by simply stating how it makes you feel and what it makes you want to do. Ask they child if that is the affect that they are looking for. If they answer no, suggest some other solutions. If they say yes, I strongly suggest you move to consequence 705 above.
707. With older children, I have found it helpful to say some small thing like "Oh, a baby face." It usually gets anger and denial which is an opening to discuss how adults handle things they don't like.

ADD METHODS YOU HAVE USED:

_____
_____
_____
_____

Finicky Eater

These are for children that are *willing* to cooperate in consequences.

708. Make a deal that you will provide at least one thing at dinner that they like if they will eat one bite of something they do not like.
709. Try setting in some sort of a reward for trying to eat some food that they are not too found of; a sweet or a special privilege because they are choosing to take care of themselves.
710. I have had very good results with allowing the child to be part of the preparation or getting the food. Once I had a person who hated vegetables become a real fan of them after starting to garden.
711. Try to come up with what the real problem is. Is the taste too bland, do they dislike a mushy texture. Often you can cancel out a fair amount of old prejudices, by using new preparation methods.
712. Work with a nutritional chart. Have the child themselves plan how they are going to get the food groups they need and make sure they are aware of the outcomes for them if they don't.

These are for children that are *unwilling* to cooperate in consequences.

713. Sometimes you can burn a person out on a food by giving them all that they want of it in a short time period. I had a child who would kick at anything but hamburgers. After about two weeks straight of them she was asking me for something else. The trick here is not to give too much variation at other times
714. Ignore the behavior but simply set in reward for the right behavior. Such as anyone who eats their dinner gets ice cream. That makes it the child's choice.
715. Make the portions you give the child small. If the child eats all of that, they can have seconds. Hunger remains the best appetite increaser.
716. Allow the child to choose what they want for one meal, but then everyone else gets to choose what they want for another. To get the choice, they must eat a little of what everyone else chooses.
717. Ignore the behavior entirely. Give the child lots of praise when they do practice eating everything. Manipulate the environment so the child is getting some meals they like or this will be ineffective.

ADD METHODS YOU HAVE USED:

_____
_____
_____
_____

Fearful Behavior

This behavior probably is best colored in greens. Ranging in the pale lemon greens of a nagging doubt on a test one has to take, going into the deep forest green of an inability to take any sort of a risk at all. Fear, like all other emotions is good, and God given. It tells us we need to look before we leap. It slows us down and makes us wise. None of us want our children to be so fearful of the decisions life calls on them to make that they never make a decision. All of us want our children to be fearful enough to use caution in the decisions they make. For myself, I want my children to slow down, get wise advice then move on as they feel is best. The result of that is going to be poor decisions, sometimes. I try very hard as a parent, not to put so much emphasis on them failing, that I overlook the fact they took a step in faith and the good aspects of the step. The whole removal of extreme fear is a building of faith. Whether that faith is in their God, or in themselves, or in the community at large, it is the faith that propels them forward into action; when we keep in mind, that this is the real moving power that will overcome the behaviors, our actions become much more positive and encouraging. I also realize that from a fear powered person, often the only thing that will move them is something they fear more. In this simple understanding comes a world of knowledge. If I wish the child to take an action often all I have to do is feed into one of their greater fears.

I had a child that was really frightened of taking a test at school. The fear of the test had her not studying. The studying brought the uncomfortable knowledge that there was a test tomorrow so she chose not to study, freeing her at least momentarily from the fear. The answer to better grades and more action was this. I refused to allow the subject of the test to drop. In this way she was stuck with the discomfort whether she studied or not. I assured her that it didn't matter if she failed or passed the test. I made my only interest the fact that she was making an effort. Once the pressure was off her, she began, slowly, to not be so afraid of the tests. I think simply because it was less painful to study then to listen to me, she began to study. Once she studied she began to pass. Once she began to pass she began to enjoy studying. You can see that attacking the underlying problem can often bring the desired result. I utilized this child's fear to help her outgrow it.

Often kids can not even identify their fears, much less, overcome them. As a parent I see a large part of my job with this type of a child as helping them see what they *really* fear, and help them find ways to overcome it.

Tips to remember:
1. Fear has degrees, just like colors. Light green to forest green.
2. Fear serves a purpose, it makes us use caution.
3. Fear needs to be turned into faith.
4. Fear can often be overcome by using something one fears even more. In essence it tells you there is something too painful to face, should you continue along the path you are traveling.

Lying

These are for children that are *willing* to cooperate in consequences.

718. Sit down with the child and tell them you suspect they are lying. Let them know the consequence for the behavior you suspect. Also let them know the consequences for the lie. Give the child a choice to tell the truth and have no consequences for lying, or for you to discover the truth and the child have the consequences. Give them five minutes in their room to make a choice.
719. Have the child do a chart on the progression of lying. Have them list how one lie leads to another and another and finally, the separation of them from most people they care about.
720. Have them do a report on honesty and the spiritual benefits of it. Spend about ten minutes going over this to make sure the child understands the principles.
721. Have the child lose your trust for the day. Every time the child asks you something say, "I'm sorry I would like to believe you but I don't, because you lied to me." Act accordingly. In other words if he or she wants to go outside and play, they can only do that because you trust they will be outside, so they cannot. Be careful on how long you set in this consequence for, as it will take you a lot of time to monitor. Better an hour you can monitor than a day you cannot.
722. If the lying is more story telling, retell the story. In other words, go over what you think is fabrication saying the truth and explain that nothing "great" has to happen for you to be interested in them.

These are for children that are *unwilling* to cooperate in consequences.

723. Have a **family meeting** and preset the consequences for lying. These are to be decided by the group which eliminates a lot of fear of telling the truth.
724. Set in no consequence for the behavior if the child tells you the truth. This rewards honesty and encourages close family relationships. Only one caution here, make it clear that telling the truth *just before* you are going to discover it anyway, is **NOT** being truthful.
725. Make the consequence for the behavior increased by half if the child has lied about it. For example, the consequence for going over to a friend's house without permission, is that the child can't see the friend for one day. The child tells you your spouse gave permission and they didn't. The child cannot go to the friends for a day and a half. Half a day for lying and a day for going there at all.
726. Ignore the lie and focus on the truth. In other words, say, "Well, I do believe this and the other in your story." Use silence to make the child sort through your reaction. If the child goes to leave, simply say, "We are not done discussing this so it will come up again." Make sure it does.
727. Make a statement of fact. "You and I both know that is not the truth. Now here is what I am going to do about this behavior." Take care on this that you are sure you are correct, otherwise you are doing no different than the child.

ADD METHODS YOU HAVE USED:

_____
_____
_____

Making Impulsive Decisions

Realize I did not put this in the fear column by mistake. Often in our lives if we feel we cannot make a good choice or are afraid of losing some pleasure we want, we jump rather than think it out. If this becomes a habit we are people who are ruled by the feeling of the moment. Children are by nature more impulsive than adults, so you must consider that. Also, some children are hyperactive and that may need to be controlled with *medication*. However, no matter what is underlying this, I have found these consequences to help.

These are for children that are *willing* to cooperate in consequences.

728. Teach the child to have a plan for the day. Either the night before or in the morning plan out the day with them. Do not make the plans for them; simply help them put it in order.
729. Have the child do a ten count before the action. I like to have them do ten deep breathes then go on with what they plan to do.
730. Have them do a little thing I call **SODA** out loud. Start with the last letter of the word; A-ction, that I want to take. D-isadvantanges, to doing it. O-ptions, that I may not have considered. S-olution, that I have come up with. This teaches the child to think through their plans.
731. Have the child give you some reasons why the action might not work out before they leave. Try to allow the child to experience both the successes and failures of their choices if possible. Keep your focus on praising their "thinking it out."
732. Let the child monitor their own thought process through a chart. On the chart, mark the times when the child thought about what they were going to do and the outcome. Then the times they didn't and the outcome.

These are for children that are *unwilling* to cooperate in consequences.

733. Most of the above have worked with even *unwilling* children, but to encourage them, you can use some tools like: "You can go out as soon as you give me two minutes of thinking time."
734. List the options that the child may not have considered. Then tell them they can continue as soon as they give you either a new option, or can tell you two of the ones you gave them.
735. Ask the child why? Then say, "OK, go do it." This has been extremely effective for me since it requires the child to slow down enough to verbalize and also teaches that thinking about a thing doesn't necessarily mean not doing it. The thing I need to watch is that I don't only ask when I have concerns, because that *reinforces* the idea that if the child thinks it out they won't be able to do it.
736. Dream build. Before bed or some other quiet time put on soft music and allow for quiet and calm. Let the child know how your thoughts are roaming. Ask them how theirs are going, but don't insist on an answer. The true goal is to teach the child they can deal with quiet and no stimulation.

ADD METHODS YOU HAVE USED:
_____
_____
_____
_____

Stealing Food

These are for children that are *willing* to cooperate in consequences.

737. Allow for choices in their eating time and products, conditional on the food not being stolen. A good example would be, I allow $2.00 a week for breakfast items. They can only choose that item as long as I don't find other items missing.
738. Have a plan. If there is a certain food they are stealing or a certain time they are stealing it, come up with an alternative way to meet the child's need. I had a child who had night cravings. We resolved the problem by setting aside a small snack that was allowable.
739. Talk to the child about eating as an addiction. Discuss some of the consequences that will result from it being an ongoing problem. By confronting, you will make the child aware of the price they may pay for the continuation of the behavior.
740. Make the kitchen off limits for the day. Tell them unless they respect the items in the kitchen, then they will lose the privilege of being in the kitchen.
741. Require the child to make a food chart planning what they are going to eat and when. Try to make it as positive an experience as possible. Take time to go over it once a week and see how they are doing. Place the emphasis on *them* owning the food rather than allowing the food to own them.

These are for children that are *unwilling* to cooperate in consequences.

742. Stop buying the item that is being stolen for a couple of weeks. Soda is a real big temptation in our house. I buy three liters a week for meals. If the soda doesn't last, the next week it's kool-aid. Be sure the child is aware of why you are not buying the item this time.
743. You can lock the cabinets or refrigerator. I know of many parents who do this, but it is a choice I don't prefer. I have found it hard to monitor and seems to *challenge* the offender to "break in."
744. Have them repay the amount plus five dollars, by doing without some snack or extra item they normally have. I always explain that, "X amount of money buys X amount of items." If they take an item, then it must be replaced from somewhere.
745. Pre-teach. Go over all the items and tell the child not to touch them as you know they are there. Every time they head for the kitchen say, "What are you after?" Get it in your mind to start giving trust back every day that nothing disappears

ADD METHODS YOU HAVE USED:

_____
_____
_____
_____

Clinging to You

I had to realize a certain amount of clinging at young ages is normal and healthy. I am talking about the child who will not face life experiences and uses you almost as a shield to living.

These are for children that are *willing* to cooperate in consequences.

746. Set in a cuddle time. Explain to the child that this is the time you are going to allow them to cling. Any other clinging to them will be subtracted from that time.
747. Sit the child down and explain how the behavior makes you feel. Have them practice little acts of courage. An example is a child who clings to you when you try and introduce them to a friend. Practice by having a friend the child knows over and going through the introduction process three or four times.
748. Set up a plan for individuality. I am going to send you in to talk to your teacher alone because I want you to learn how to be independent. I will come in then and we will talk to her together.
749. Have the child *earn* the right to cling by doing the uncomfortable thing first. Danny you may hang onto me after you have introduced yourself to Mrs. Jones.
750. Pre-teach. Tell the child what is going to happen and the behavior you expect. Have the child tell you how they are planning on acting. You might even try rehearsing it, giving the child lots of praise.

These are for children that are *unwilling* to cooperate in consequences.

751. You can set in a time limit for clinging to you. You may cling to me until I count to ten and then I will remove you and walk away if I need to.
752. You can place yourself in such a way to make the clinging next to impossible for the child to get to you. You will need to think out where you are locating yourself before you do something that might get the child to cling.
753. Address the clinging in clear uncertain terms. You do not enjoy the behavior. It makes you feel trapped and you do not want the child to do it. This seems to work the best for me if I do not smile and make my voice tone firm. I like to go back later and explain why, rather than risk the child thinking I don't like them.
754. Do not let it work. Behind the clinging is either something the child does not want to face or something the child wants. If it is something that they want, find another way that they can get it. If it is something they don't want, make sure they have to do it. Basically, make sure the clinging doesn't work.
755. Offer a reward for the appropriate behavior. "You showed so much independence in that matter and didn't cling to me, how about you choose the TV show? Looks like you are becoming adult enough to have more choices."

ADD METHODS YOU HAVE USED:

_____
_____
_____
_____

Won't Go to School

I am speaking here of the child with an ongoing fear of school and the various parts of it—a test, the other children, etc. Do hold in your mind some of the things going on today in schools are frightening, so don't act as if there is nothing to fear if there really is. Check out your child's reasons.

These are for children that are *willing* to cooperate in consequences.
756. Sit with the child and help them identify what they are afraid of. This is pretty easy to do if you break it down into small times and address the symptoms the child is feeling. When you go to the bus do you feel like you have to go to the bathroom? Do you still feel like you want to throw up while in your first period class? The symptoms will disappear after the child has faced the situation. You can then make a plan to help them face the problem.
757. Build in a support group. I understand that you feel afraid, how about talking to the child next door and you plan on going together and helping each other for the next week.
758. Get the child to agree to go in for the first hour then to call you if they feel like they cannot handle it. If they call, try first to get the fear identified and take action. If they still are unwilling or unable to go a step further, agree to let them go for a soda if they will then return to school. Check with the teacher whose class the child missed to make sure they are not avoiding some problem.
759. Build in some pleasure base for school. I'll drive you to the bus stop if you'll take it from there. I'll see you get in volleyball if you will continue to try and go in.
760. Build in faith. Set aside a few minutes in the morning to read (to or with) the child on spiritual reading based on faith. I have found the idea of a guardian angel standing right there to protect them is extremely effective. Kids have vivid imaginations and it appeals to that. I once had one of my grandchildren tell her mother when frightened by a robbery she had witnessed, "Let's go over to Grandma's house that's where the big angels live."

1001 NATURAL LOGICAL CONSEQUENCES

These are for children that are *unwilling* to cooperate in consequences.

761. Go to the guidance counselor. Take the child with you and share the child's concerns. Have the guidance counselor plan a time for the child to stop in and make sure all is going well.
762. Plan a parent teacher conference. Share what is going on with the child and have the teacher monitor the behavior at school to see if the problem can be identified.
763. Take five minutes after school to talk about the child's school day. Focus **ONLY** on what was right. How brave they were to go and all they overcame that day. Continue to do that until the talk of not wanting to go to school subsides.
764. Every time the child comes to you with a fear of going in, point out at least four things they did right at school the last time they went and assure them they can handle it. Tell them they are welcome to call if they get there and are still afraid.
765. If the child simply will not go, offer to take them and if they refuse tell them you will be forced to have the police pick them up and bring them in because the law requires they go. Use this as a **last** resort and try to remain empathetic, but out of choices.

ADD METHODS YOU HAVE USED:

_____
_____
_____
_____

Chronic Complaining

These are for children that are *willing* to cooperate in consequences.

766. Have the child tell four positive aspects of the item or object that they are complaining about.
767. Set in a complaint box. All complaints must be written and put in the box to be discussed at the **family meeting**. Make sure that they are discussed, but ask the person first, is this still a problem or have you resolved it. Be sure to build in positives if it has been resolved.
768. Help the child process. Make a statement such as "Oh, so what do you think would be the best way to resolve that?" No matter *how* the child responds, praise the effort to resolve it. If you get an inappropriate choice such as punch his lights out, let the child know you also have felt that way, but what does the child think the outcome of such an act would be, do they want that outcome? What might be some other choices?
769. Set aside a time each day for complaints. I have found if they get no attention from anyone else the child is likely to resolve them rather then wait in discomfort until the appointed time. I have also found I have to remind the child that they are complaining and it is not complaint time.

These are for children that are *unwilling* to cooperate in consequences.

770. Work as a secretary. When the child complains just ask them to wait a minute and grab a pencil and paper. Write down the complaint and say these sound like some good issues for our **family meeting**.
771. Make a statement of fact. "Do you know complaining is a way of saying you are not smart enough to solve the problem? I simply don't believe that is true."
772. Another statement I often use is, "A problem is only the start of a miracle. If you handle it God's way you will have something wonderful happen at the end of it." This focuses the child on resolve rather than complaining.
773. Ignore the behavior completely. Make a statement like, "Oh, really," and just turn the conversation to something else. You might choose to bring a few of these things up at the **family meeting** to show you heard and care. It might also give you some great positives for the child in the area of problem solving.
774. Point out some solutions. Take care on this that the child doesn't see you as the problem solver or you will get more problems to solve. You can point out some solutions that might work and let the child have the choice. I personally like to add one real poor choice to help the child see that I am not God in giving answers.
775. Have a God box. If the child complains, offer to pray with him or pray for them, then put the written problem in the God box. Open it once a month to see how God is doing. Don't be like me and try to help God fix it or you will get the wrong effect.

ADD METHODS YOU HAVE USED:
_____
_____

Agrees with Everyone

Being agreeable is a great character trait. When a child takes it to the extreme, it becomes *people pleasing* and could get them into all kinds of hot water. I refer here to children who are very frightened of disagreement with anyone.

These are for children that are *willing* to cooperate in consequences.

776. Have the child practice saying no, no thanks, not today, in the mirror every day. This will build in feeling comfortable with no. Don't be surprised if you are the first one they practice on. Praise their taking a stand, but let them know the price for non-compliance. If you can, let this type of a child win, by accepting if possible, their no.
777. Help your child know their own boundaries by having them go over why they agree with some things. "I heard you tell Jill abortion was ok. I'm not disagreeing or agreeing I simply was wondering why you felt that way and if you had enough facts to make an informed decision."
778. Build in strength by confronting where the child was double minded and playing sides with the child involved. An example is the child who normally chooses to do chores, but agrees with a friend that it is cool to dodge chores. Play first the part of the child taking a stand, next be the person agreeing. Have your child be the other child. Ask her which felt better.
779. Plan in activities that require taking a position and sticking to it. Such a game might be truth or consequences. Scruples is another game that requires you to think out and stand true to a position. Help the child see that this is a good rather than a bad thing.
780. Have the child look at both statements and teach them how to make an informed judgment. Have them go back to the person they were just agreeing with and say, "You know I hadn't really thought about this when you asked me, but I have since thought about it and this is what I really feel.

These are for children that are *unwilling* to cooperate in consequences.

781. Hold true to boundaries that you have heard the child set. If you heard them say that Jimmy is a jerk. The next time they want to go to Jimmy's tell them, "No, I heard you saying Jimmy is a jerk, and I believed you, so I don't think it is a good place to be." Be sure to give the child a way out by offering to change your mind if they say they were wrong and agree not to do it again.
782. Write down the two statements that the child is saying and who they are saying them to. Wait for a calm moment and read them to the child. Ask which one is the truth. Point out that others cannot trust them when they give different stories.
783. Share your own experience with trying to be all things to all people and the outcome of them. Allow the child to see that in most cases both of the people you were trying to please were upset at you. Don't be afraid to point out the similarities in what you see going on in the child's life.
784. Confront the problem in front of the other person. Say, "I couldn't help overhearing you say you don't believe in God, yet, I heard you tell Mike last week you did, I'm confused which is it?" This works best for me if the person present is the one I am pretty sure the child is trying to impress.

ADD METHODS YOU HAVE USED:

_____
_____
_____
_____

Won't Make Decisions

This is the child you find you are always having to do for, or being blamed for the outcome of actions because you somehow were convinced that they needed you to tell them how to handle it.

These are for children that are *willing* to cooperate in consequences.

785. Sit down with the child and tell them that you realize you have been taking their choices away from them. Explain that from then on, you will be offering them options and that the decision is theirs as is the outcome of it.
786. Have the child go over the word decide, which means "to cut in half." Help them become aware that even a bad decision is half as easy as no decision.
787. Get a book on decision making. Have the child read it and have a mini test. Allow the child to practice decision making by prompting them with real situations you have seen them struggle with.
788. Work with options. When the child comes to you say, "These are your options as I see them." Be sure to stress that only the child can make the decision and only they can be responsible for the outcome.

These are for children that are *unwilling* to cooperate in consequences.

789. Focus on the positive. Note the decisions that the child is making and point them out. Also point out the positive outcomes, or allow time for the child to tell them to you.
790. Refuse to make the decision for the child. If that means nothing happens, then so be it. Later, point out that the child's indecision brought the outcome into being.
791. Play a game I call the **thinking, feeling, doing game**. I use it in the car and the game consists of asking a person a life situation then either what do you feel, think, or do. The person has the right to pass but if they answer, they get to ask the next question. And the person who asks gets to go again. With this type of child, focus many of your questions into what do you do. Thus, pre-teaching in a fun way.
792. Focus on the outcomes. In other words say, "You made a choice whether you know it or not, and this was the outcome of that choice. If you would like more control over your outcomes start making more of your choices." This works very well if the child moves from you making their choices, to school friends making them.

ADD METHODS YOU HAVE USED:

_____
_____
_____
_____
_____

Has Anxiety Attacks

These are for children that are *willing* to cooperate in consequences.

793. I think one of the most effective things is to have the child take breaks. Let them do a small part, then walk outside, close their eyes, and take five deep breaths. Then go do five more minutes and repeat again. I have found the most fearful situation can be overcome this way.
794. Have the child put it in the *now*. You will need to work with them on this. I am only going to the door, I am only walking in, I am only talking to the doctor. I am only watching him fill the needle. This will allow the second of fear to be manageable and hopefully overcome the terror.
795. Give the child choices; dentists use this often. Allow them to tell you when they want to stop. Rest a bit, refuse to talk about what they are panicking over then say, "OK let's try a little more."
796. Use prayer. When we feel our own resources are not enough we will often find comfort in the strength of another larger Being. Teach your child to utilize this and offer to pray with them.
797. Teach the child guided imagery. "I am going to leave this scary place and in my mind go visit a charming prince in a castle. Can you see him? Close your eyes and tell me what he looks like." Move their mind away from what they need to face.

These are for children that are *unwilling* to cooperate in consequences.

798. You do the breakdown. Part of the problem is we want to get control of the whole situation in the moment. Don't do that. Stop and offer to hold the child for a moment. After that ask if they are afraid to walk to the car, stop once in the car and ask if they are afraid to let you drive. Continue to walk the child a little at a time.
799. Give a firm command. "You may not choose to go, but then I will have to call the doctor and he will call an ambulance and it will only be more frightening. Won't you help me to help you?" You can use the police or whatever fits.
800. Stop and allow the child to say, "No, I won't agree with them." Next, ask them what will happen if the child does that, then follow it out. Often the child will talk themselves out of it.
801. Stop and start to pray out loud. The child will ask what you are doing or if they don't, tell them. Explain you know they cannot do this thing alone and you are calling on the angels (or God or your concept) to help and protect them. When you are done, in a matter of fact way say, "Ok let's go, we want to see how you'll be protected. Maybe the doctor will have been called away."

ADD METHODS YOU HAVE USED:

_____
_____
_____
_____

Won't Go to Bed

These are for children that are *willing* to cooperate in consequences.

802. If the child is not in bed by bedtime, lower the bedtime the same amount of time the child is up the next day. If the bedtime is eight o'clock and the child doesn't get to bed until eight thirty, the next night bedtime is seven thirty.
803. Hold a **family meeting** and ask the child what the problem is. Make the solution to the problem dependant on going to bed on time. I get afraid in the dark, might bring, "You can have a light on if you are in bed by eight o'clock."
804. Have the child make a list of all things that are on their mind and put the list in the drawer for the night. This is a physical thing they can do to unburden themselves.
805. If the problem is safety oriented, have the child lock the doors and check the windows before bed. Teach them some prayer that is of protection through the night. I like having the invisible covering of Christ cover the house, and or the angels standing guard at every door and window.
806. If the child is just stalling, have the child make a list or tell you everything they are going to need before bed. Do this an hour before bedtime. Next, line up all the things and anything else that the child wants is simply not on your list, but you can write it on tomorrows list.

These are for children that are *unwilling* to cooperate in consequences.

807. Allow bedtimes to be raised by observing promptness when going to bed. In other words, if a bedtime is eight o'clock the only way it can get to nine o'clock is by being in bed by eight.
808. If the child enjoys light or music at bedtime, take either one out of the room and let the child know that if they are in bed on time, the item will be returned.
809. Set in a snack and sharing time. Often the child does not know how to free themselves from the cares of the day and thus fall to sleep. Take ten minutes before their bedtime to let them settle down and share their day.
810. Reward the child's going to bed on time or anywhere near the bedtime verbally. Such a comment might be, "You almost have this getting to bed on time down, we better start thinking about how you are going to spend that extra half hour."
811. Darken the whole house for a half an hour at the child's bedtime. Explain that you and the others need quiet also, so the whole house will be darkened. Usually, if you do this it will take half an hour before you can resume life in the front rooms.

ADD METHODS YOU HAVE USED:

_____
_____
_____
_____

Has Nightmares

Nightmares can be a normal part of childhood; a way for the mind to release the fears that a child builds up during the day. If however, they are constant or ongoing, action should be taken to ensure that there is not another cause. Get *professional help* if this is the case.

These are for children that are *willing* to cooperate in consequences.

812. Set aside a comforting play time or story time the last half of an hour before bed. Strive for things that are reassuring to the child.
813. Bring it up in a **family meeting**. Have the other members share what helps them when they have had a bad dream. Have the child make some decisions about what they will do the next time it happens.
814. Sit with the child and go over the reading material, games and TV shows they are watching. Eliminate all that are of a frightening nature. Give the child suggestions as to what they could replace it with.
815. Have the child watch what they are eating before bedtime. Certain foods are inclined to bring on nightmares. Have them eat something bland or creamy.
816. Have the child role play out the dream once they are awake. Have them finish it with an ending that saves them.

These are for children that are *unwilling* to cooperate in consequences.

817. Do a room check. Since this type of a child probably cannot express what they are afraid of, watch closely for what seems to comfort them. Look in closets, under beds, and all around make sure the windows are secure and reassure them they are safe.
818. Remove from the child any videos, music tapes, or books that could be of a fearful nature during the evening hours. Note the Bedtime stories you are reading. If they are Fire and Brimstone, God killed them or something similar, exchange them for some more nurturing ones.
819. Set in house rules as to what to do when you wake up in the middle of the night afraid. Even an uncooperative child will often remember and use them. I like, (check that all the doors are locked, check windows, sit and have a glass of milk, go back to bed and redo our prayers).
820. When the child is retelling the dream, encourage them to give a positive outcome. If the child is unwilling, try building in what you think the child might do if it really happened. Try not to discount the dream. Instead of a statement like, "You know there are no monsters," say, "Sounds scary, but I bet if that really happened you could get a stick and beat them off."

ADD METHODS YOU HAVE USED:
_____
_____
_____
_____

Can't Sleep

Like the child who has nightmares a certain amount of this is normal growing up behavior. I speak of a continued problem. Don't forget the value of "white noise" to help a child fall asleep.

These are for children that are *willing* to cooperate in consequences.

821. Confront the problem at a **family meeting**. Have each member state something they do when they are having trouble sleeping. Allow the child to choose one of the tools and see how it works for a week. Check on progress at the next **family meeting**. If it is not working have the child try a different one.
822. Have the child be aware of what they are eating two hours before bedtime. Eliminate any thing with a heavy chocolate or sugar base. Have them replace it with a milk type product.
823. Set aside a half an hour reading time. Use something rather restful and non exciting. I like a repetitious book like Numbers in the bible but an encyclopedia will also do. This will tire the child's eyes and make sleep easier.
824. Putting on a talk show on TV or radio half an hour before bed can have the same affect; something that the child will find dull. Be sure to turn the lights down.
825. If you are pretty sure the problem is deliberate on the child's part, you set their bedtime or wake up time to the lesser or greater. If you wish to get them up earlier, explain you are going to assume they don't need as much sleep so you are waking them. If you choose to, put them to bed earlier, explain that it seems that they take a long time to get to sleep so you are putting them to bed earlier. Take care on this because it might create a power play and that is exactly the situation you don't want.

These are for children that are *unwilling* to cooperate in consequences.

826. Set in an earlier wake up time. Monitor the child's day to make sure they are not getting their sleep during the day so that they don't want it at night.
827. Set in a lights out time. If the child is playing in their room or listening to what transpires after they are in bed, this will stop it. Usually, you can turn the lights back on about a half an hour later.
828. Ignore the behavior. However, do make the child aware when they have fallen asleep at an earlier time. I like to say something like, "I noticed you are sleeping better. What have you been doing? I sure do find that very responsible."
829. Monitor their bedtime activities such as bath, nightclothes bed clean. Explain that there must be a reason that they are not sleeping and you, as their parent, are responsible to find out what it is. This works very well with older children since independence is so important to them.

ADD METHODS YOU HAVE USED:

_____
_____
_____
_____

Making up Wild Stories

These are for children that are *willing* to cooperate in consequences.

830. Confront the child. Ask them to go back over the details. Walk through the situation with the child if they seem sure of how it happened. Encourage the child to talk to their friend about how *they* saw it.
831. Explain to the child when they tell you things like that it breaks your trust in them. The next time the child wants to go and do a similar thing, tell them that your trust was broken by the story they told.
832. Have the child write down the story explaining that you are having trouble believing them. Wait for a week and pull the story out of where you have put it, reading it back to the child. Ask them to tell you now if it doesn't sound foolish to them. Try to get them to be honest. If they are, don't assume it.
833. Have the child tell you five reasons why exaggerating might not be a good idea. If it is an older child you might want them to write it and bring the topic up at the **family meeting**. If a younger child, you will need to help by walking through the steps you might take if you believed them.

These are for children that are *unwilling* to cooperate in consequences.

834. Confront the child saying that you doubt that is really what happened although it may be what they believe happened. Go back and check with other people involved or bring the child to where they say it occurred.
835. Ignore it. Tell the child those kind of stories do not really interest you because you have trouble believing them. Just as important, try to pay a lot of attention to the little every day things. Reinforcing how much you appreciate their honesty.
836. Set in a story time for a week or so. During that time the child can make up stories and you will listen. This gives the child an outlet for their imagination and still concretes them into this is not true. Do not engage in a battle over this is true or not, simply say this would be better told at our story time.
837. Wait, and later that day you tell the child a story with strongly added fantasy. Once you are done and the child's reaction is doubt, explain that this is how you feel when they tell you stories like they did earlier. Be sure to let the child know the truth and that it would be ok with you if they didn't tell you the truth earlier, to tell you now.

ADD METHODS YOU HAVE USED:

_____
_____
_____
_____

Vehicle Misuse, the Daily Roller Coaster

I have chosen to color this behavior orange that seems to fit because it is a combination of both anger and careless behavior. Like most combined behaviors it can have several goals. The child might truly find this fun. A combination of the power they gain from your fear and the natural excitement that comes when they take risks. Like the color chart it may have a range of either anger or excitement. It may be the almost orange-red of the angry child who tries to open the door of the car in a fit of rage, to the lemon orange of the child who hangs out the window to scream at a stranger for the thrill it provides. Either way, it makes a nightmare out of the thought of traveling for the parents. That was why I called it a roller coaster ride. When faced on a daily basis it becomes something like an adventure into the unknown in a moving vehicle. This is not an underlying emotion, but a combination of emotions that are coming out in a directed way. You, as a parent, are probably the best equipped to discover what is the underlying emotion. I personally, have found that vehicle misbehavior centers on the fact that in this place, the child can feel both absolute power and control. They can get what they want and get it then. The desired result for the parent will often be in after the fact consequences, and in changing the child's thinking on how much is to be gained versus the cost involved. If the underlying emotion is anger, then you will need to find more suitable ways for the child to express it. If it is excitement you will need to find safer means for the child to fill that need. Both will respond well to *consequences*, but you will have to find a place where the child can fill the need they have, or the behavior will reoccur in a different form.

Misuse while traveling is a big danger. Also, the danger of trying to confront it on the road is very real. More than one accident has happened because an irate parent was trying to solve a problem in the mist of trying to maneuver a car. For that reason, if for no other, I strongly suggest that you pull off the road before attempting to handle any problem—if you are late, then so be it, at least you will get there alive.

The second thing I would like to stress is that many of these behaviors do **not** need immediate attention. If it is one that does not, wait until a time set up for handling such things or at least until you get off the road. In an effort to help you do that, most of these consequences will be delayed. This is one where the more you can hold in the front of your head "How strong is the need to handle this now?" the more successful you will be. I also find that pre-teaching and taking the proper precautions is a Godsend in such cases. If you feel the problem is coming, handle it before you get in the car. I have listed much in that area. Either way it is a real danger and you have every right to get that knot in your stomach the minute someone talks about going somewhere. That assures you that your feelings are not crazy.

Tips to remember:
1. Vehicle misuse is a combination of emotions.
2. It is colored orange to represent anger and carelessness.
3. It is a real danger.
4. By realizing the child's motives I can use other means to meet the child's need.
5. It is best handled before or after the fact.
6. I need to hold in mind, is this something I **must** handle now?
7. Pull off the road and arrive alive.

Taking Car Without Permission

These are for children that are *willing* to cooperate in consequences.

838. If the child has a driver's license, and often uses the car, you can take the use of the car away for a week. If they do not have a license, you can make allowing them in the car off limits for a week. Be careful that you do not box yourself in and that there is nowhere you must take them for a week.
839. Have them call a rental car agency and find out the normal rental fee of a car. Have the child pay that amount plus an added day of chores to make up for the time you had to waste worrying.
840. Have the child do a report on the consequences of unauthorized use of a vehicle. Follow that with a contract on times of use and ownership of the vehicle.
841. Explain that since the child seemed unable to differentiate from who owned the vehicle this month they can be responsible for the costs, car payment, insurance, gas, and cleaning. This will seem severe so you are welcome to figure those cost's into the hours the child used it.
842. Have the child make up a schedule for the rest of the week or month stating when they hope to borrow the car. Revise it to your schedule and then remove one or two times to make up for the time they took it without permission. Do not allow the child to vary from it or it will become ineffective. Better a week you can say no to—then a month you can't.

These are for children that are *unwilling* to cooperate in consequences.

843. Lock your car and your keys up in a safe place. Each time the child wants to go somewhere for the next week or so delay leaving, saying how much trouble it is to get out the keys.
844. Call the police. It is not a serious crime, but I think many parents are afraid to prosecute their children thinking it is. The police pulling them over will have a lasting impact on them.
845. Remove all rights to the car for a set time period. You can choose that by your schedule and how hard it will be on you to enforce it. Have the child ride a bike to the functions she or he would normally drive to.
846. If this is an ongoing problem or your child does not have the right to drive, have an alarm installed in your car or take out one of the spark plugs when you are not going to be around. Basically, prevent the event from having a chance of reoccurring. At the same time, withhold vehicle privileges to reimburse you for the time the child had it.

ADD METHODS YOU HAVE USED:
_____
_____
_____
_____

Refusing to Stay in the Seat Belt

These are for children that are *willing* to cooperate in consequences.

847. Hold a **family meeting** and discuss the importance of seat belts. Have the child give the reasons why they are getting out of them. Try to meet whatever need they are expressing. *They are uncomfortable*, offer a cloth they can put in between them and the seat belt. *I can't see out the window*, offer window seat or divide time up on who has window seat.
848. Have the child write ten times "I will not take off my seat belt," for every time they take it off. This can be done at home and younger children can say it.
849. Pull the car off the road and have the child get out and stretch before you are willing to get back on the road, let them know this is because they took the seatbelt off. Also, if they take it off again you plan on doing it again. This works best if it is someplace *they* want to go rather than someplace *you* want to go.
850. Have the child put together a play box of favorite things to do. Do not go out without reminding them to take it. Explain that they will lose it if the seatbelt comes off. If they take it off, take the box for the remainder of the ride.
851. Place a string or cloth tied to the seatbelt after the child is in the belt to help act as a reminder to stay in it. Explain to the child that this is because they continue to unbuckle it and if they can give you three trips staying in the seatbelt you will remove it.

These are for children that are *unwilling* to cooperate in consequences.

852. Explain to the child that you are going to start pulling over when they get out of their seatbelt. When you pull over observe complete silence. Wait for them to put on the seatbelt before continuing.
853. Create a car box. Put in it coloring books, crayons, and other small toys for the children to use. Put it in the front and allow the children to play with it only as long as they are in their seatbelts. If they get out of their seatbelts, either remove it from them or don't allow them to have it on the next ride.
854. The next time the child wants to go somewhere tell them that you can't take them because you are afraid they won't stay in their seatbelt. Put the power in the child's hands by asking them what they plan to do to make you feel safe driving them. Accept the consequence *they* come up with.
855. Before you get into the car with the child, go over the behavior you expect. Have the child repeat your expectations back to you. Remind them of the last time, asking what they plan on doing different this time. Be sure there is a concrete game plan before entering the car.
856. The next time the child wants to go somewhere do not allow them to get right into the car. Instead, make them walk to the corner. Explain that since they won't use seatbelts you feel they are going to need a lot of practice walking. Keep your voice tone even or they will perceive this as a power struggle and the behavior will escalate.

ADD METHODS YOU HAVE USED:

_____
_____
_____
_____

Distracting Behavior in Car

This can be anything from constant, "Look at this," to loud radios, or fighting with a sibling. Here are some very good "catch all" consequences.

These are for children that are *willing* to cooperate in consequences.
857. Hold a **family meeting** and put in preventative measures. Set guidelines and post them on the back seat of the car. Be sure to give the children things they can do instead. An example would be, (No asking the driver to look at other than the road), you can tell them you wish to show them something as soon as the car stops.
858. Once the car starts, build in a road game. Some good examples might be the alphabet game where each person takes a letter in rotation and tries to find something starting with that letter. For instance you have A-Al, the child has b-Bob. Another is to try and find the alphabet in the first letter of road signs; a-Atlanta, b-Broadway, etc.
859. Utilize the radio. If behavior is within the guidelines the first few minutes, the child gets to choose the radio station they want to listen to. If you have more than one child, give one the choice on the way there and one the choice on the way back.
860. Once you get back home, have the child list the distracting behavior and also two choices for what they could have done instead. Post that in the back of the car and when the behavior starts to reappear just remind the child to look at the list.
861. Have a toy box—a small box of things to do in the car. Keep it in the car and **DO NOT** allow the children to use it at any other time. This keeps it a novel thing to them. Allow them only one item at a time and only as long as they do not distract anyone.

These are for children that are *unwilling* to cooperate in consequences.

862. Make the front seat a privilege. As long as the rules are obeyed they can ride in the front seat. You can do that with several children by: following the rules the number of days you have children, earns you the front seat one day.
863. Pre-teach *before* you start the car, going over the rules. Explain to the child that you will stop doing this as soon as you are sure they know them and you will know that by their behavior. If the child says that they do know them have them tell them to you.
864. Pull the car over to the side of the road and have the child tell you what they want. After they are finished explain that this may make you both late and that you would prefer they handle these things at home. This works best if you are bringing the child somewhere *they* want to go.
865. When a distraction starts, turn off the radio. Explain that you cannot listen to them and the radio at the same time. Oddly enough, this works particularly well with teens. They quickly get the idea they can have your attention or the radio.
866. Take away the choice of where they sit in the car. Simply tell them they are distracting you, pull the car over to the side of the road and refuse to drive any further until they switch seats; putting the distracting child furthest away from you. An exception you need to note is if your child gets physically violent **do not** place him or her in the back seat where they might grab you from behind.

ADD METHODS YOU HAVE USED:
_____
_____
_____

Opens Car Door When Moving

This is a *dangerous* behavior and needs to be handled as such.

These are for children that are *willing* to cooperate in consequences.
867. Immediately pull the car over to the side of the road. Put on the child proof locks. Put the child in the back seat if they are not already there. Keep your voice tone serious and explain that that has cost them the privilege of the front seat for at least two weeks.
868. Have the child call the police station and find out the laws pertaining to opening a car door when the car is moving and the possible risks. Have them give you a written report on it. If it is a small child, bring them down and let the police talk to them about it. Review it when you get home.
869. Bring the child to your local hospital—call first to see if there are any car accident victims. Let the child meet them. Explain to the child the same thing could have happened to the both of you.
870. Get a video tape from the police or local library showing auto accidents. Explain to the child the danger and how easily that could have happened when they opened the door. Be sure to help them realize this is a real thing happening since movies can build in a sort of unreal affect.

These are for children that are *unwilling* to cooperate in consequences.

871. Put on child proof locks and make the back seat mandatory for at least two weeks. Let the child know this is very dangerous and needs extremely protective devices.
872. Pre-teach. At least once a day for the next few weeks let the child know how they frightened you and how easily they could have been hurt by doing that.
873. Make the car off limits for the week. Let the child know that the opening of the door has worried you so much that you simply don't feel safe driving him anywhere for the next week.
874. Only allow the child to ride in the car for the next week if there is someone else besides you to grab them should they open the car door. Be sure to place them in the back with the other person. Also, put the responsibility on them to ask another person to come, explaining why they need them there.
875. Bring your minister or other people the child respects over and tell them what happened. Let them know the child really worried you and ask if they will talk to them.

ADD METHODS YOU HAVE USED:

_____
_____
_____
_____

Dangerous Bike Riding

All children like a certain amount of excitement where bike riding is concerned. I find it is often a choice of degree for safety versus the degree of risk. If it is worrying you, then act on it.

These are for children that are *willing* to cooperate in consequences.

876. Restrict the child from riding the bike for half a day. Have that moved in increments of half a day more for each offense.
877. Have the child do a written report on the rules of the road and how they could be applied in your area.
878. Have the child go to a bike riding safety class. This is likely to cost money so you will want the child to be responsible to pay for the costs. Figure something they can do without if they cannot come up with the money.
879. Pull in the boundaries where the child is allowed to ride. Each time the child observes safe riding rules allow them to earn a little of the area back.
880. Allow the child certain areas to do stunts or whatever the practice they are engaging in. Have them build a ramp in the yard or take them to a safe spot to do the stunts. You can also become the most popular parent in the block by allowing others to help make and use these things. (Check your homeowner's insurance)

ADD METHODS YOU HAVE USED:

_____
_____
_____
_____

These are for children that are *unwilling* to cooperate in consequences.

881. Hold a **family meeting** and discuss the responsibilities of vehicles. Have each member of the family come up with some consequences that would occur if they handled things the way the child had. Ask the child which one they feel best suits their actions. If the child is unwilling to pick one, have the family vote on the most appropriate one and have the child follow through in a lesser manner. If speeding is a $25.00 fine, then perhaps the family would vote he or she should pay $5.00.

882. Make the bike disappear. Use a friend or neighbor to hold it for a few days. If you use this, offer an early release on the bike if the child will agree to one of the above consequences. Do not make it mandatory, but say, "You can have it back as soon as." Simply offer it as a choice.

883. Have a policeman or other safety official come to the house and explain the legal penalties of the child's behavior. Try to get some rules set in while you have the policeman there. If this is impossible, sit with the child later and try to get some cooperation on how to avoid you having to call them again.

884. Get a chain and a lock for the bike. If the child has misused it, have it locked the following day when they come in. Explain you would be glad to unlock it, but first they must go over the safety rules so you can be sure they won't hurt themselves. You will help the child commit them to memory by doing this the next few times they go to ride, but don't keep it up as it will get into a power play. Simply use it when misbehavior occurs.

885. Another twist on the above consequence is to use the same method, only have the child repeat 10 times they will not do whatever behavior it was that they did last time they rode the bike. I like to start with five and move up in increments of five for each time they do it.

Doesn't Obey Traffic Laws

Although this can be used for the bike rider I primarily put it in for the parents of driving children, from Mopeds, to cars.

These are for children that are *willing* to cooperate in consequences.

886. Have the child lose the privilege of driving for a day or two. Allow them to earn it back by giving you a written contract that the laws will be obeyed or they will pay you a fine.
887. Cut back the times they can drive. You may drive to and from work, but until you can practice better safety laws you will need to ride the school bus.
888. Give them practice sessions. Take a half an hour of their free time and ride with them as though they were studying for the drivers test again.
889. Have the child go back and take the practice test in the manual. Only this time let them say what they are doing. After that, have them add up the violations and the cost of them. This should build in some awareness.
890. Have them build a savings account toward the amount of the fine that will occur if they get caught. Do not forget to add in raised insurance costs. You can take a percentage of their money rather than leaving them broke.

These are for children that are *unwilling* to cooperate in consequences.

891. Report them to the police. Although they will probably not be able to ticket them you will have given the clear message that you do not approve.
892. Refuse to ride in the car with them at the wheel for a couple of weeks. Even if you don't normally let them drive when you are together it will feel like a loss of approval and also make your riding with them a privilege. Allow them to earn it back slowly by riding with them only as long as they drive safely.
893. Take the plates off the car. Explain to the child that because you are their guardian and responsible for their actions, you need to make sure the car is not misused and since you do not have their cooperation, this is a measure you must take. Offer them a way to earn it back.
894. Start withdrawing some monetary things you provide. Put this in a savings account saying that you are planning for the costs that will occur once they are caught.
895. If you pay or have the child on your insurance policy, bring them with you to the insurance company and say you are considering taking the child off the policy. Ask the agent how much you would save by doing this. Next, ask what it would cost for the child to get a separate policy. Once you are outside, let the child know that this is a direct result of their not obeying the law.

ADD METHODS YOU HAVE USED:

_____
_____
_____
_____

Grabs Things in the Car

These are for children that are *willing* to cooperate in consequences.

896. Allow them a coloring book, reading book, or some other toy to use, but only for as long as their hands remain on that and nothing else.
897. Have them write or say ten times, "I will not touch what is not mine." There is a big advantage in having them say it and that is, that the consequence becomes immediate.
898. Have the child name all the items in the car and which ones are theirs and which ones belong to someone else. Reinforce that what is not theirs; they have no right to touch.
899. Put in a penalty. Every time that the child grabs something of yours, you get to play with something of theirs, for half an hour. Do not ask the child to give it to you, go in their room and take it, letting them know that that is how you felt, because the child gave you no choice over what they would take.
900. Preplan the trip. Have the child tell you what they are going to do with the time. Let them know you don't want them grabbing things and this is a way they can help you to trust that they are people who keep their word.

ADD METHODS YOU HAVE USED:
_____
_____
_____
_____

These are for children that are *unwilling* to cooperate in consequences.

901. Pre-teach. If they grabbed the last time, do not allow them into the car until they can tell you what they are not allowed to touch. Follow this with the things they *are* allowed to touch
902. This is similar to the first, but wait until the child is in the car, drive a short way, then pull over. Say, "Oh, by the way, what things are we not going to touch during this ride?" This is quite effective with the child who likes to go running off. Do not restart the car until they have told you, or if a power struggle occurs say, "Well you must not remember so I'll tell you." Then you state which things.
903. Reinforce the positive. If the child gets in the car say thanks for not grabbing. Every few minutes phrase it a little different but let them know you notice and are appreciative.
904. Chart the behavior. For each five minutes that they didn't touch something that was not theirs, give five minutes of travel time. An example would be Tony wants to go to the store. The first five minutes buys him the next five minutes until you get to the store. If he touches something you need to go home or he needs to walk the rest of the way. To keep from boxing yourself in, you might want to let the child earn five minutes by one of the willing consequences.
905. Ignore the behavior. However, be sure to reinforce the positive. Keep letting them know you appreciate the time they were doing whatever it was besides touching. Don't focus on the not touching because that still says, if I touch I get attention. Focus of whatever else it is they are doing—that says, if they do something else, they get attention.

Letting Other People Use Vehicle

I have tried to put in consequences that can work from a bicycle to a car. The truth is, if you get in the habit of letting others use your transportation you are quite likely to end up without any.

These are for children that are *willing* to cooperate in consequences.

906. Sit with the child and go over why and what happened before they loaned the vehicle. Have them replay the events leading to their loaning it. Have them go over the possible results of this action. Rehearse with them different ways they could have said "No".
907. Take the use of the vehicle away for a short time, two hours to two days. Explain that this will help them be prepared when their vehicle is damaged and they will already have built in some other skills, so it will not be as hard on them.
908. Have the child start a provisional plan with money for the probable loss of the vehicle. You can set the amount aside weekly toward when someone breaks it. Let the child know that they can stop doing that the minute they decide and can tell you how they will be saying no.
909. Have the child do a report on vehicle crimes, be sure they include the various consequences to the owner of the vehicle. Make the report age appropriate, two pages for a ten year old four for a fifteen year old. Also, if it is a bike being loaned, explain that how they handle a bike teaches you how they will handle a car.
910. Have the child tell the person they loaned it to, in front of you that they were not allowed to loan it out and they will not be letting them use it again. If you have suspicions that both children already knew this, have them do it in front of the other child's parents.

These are for children that are *unwilling* to cooperate in consequences.

911. Hold a **family meeting**. Have all the members share some of the unexpected results of loaning their vehicle to another. Have the child tell how they plan on being responsible for any of those things should they happen. Have the other family members share how they found ways to say no.

912. Make the vehicle disappear for a few days. If you choose this consequence be sure that your relationship is such that you can make the child realize the liability to you in their loaning the vehicle to others. Be clear in the fact that the frustration they are feeling is nothing compared to what they will feel if someone destroys their transportation.

913. Regain control of the vehicle by letting the child know they have it at your discretion. You may need to call officials in on this because, the common thought is, I earned it, and it is mine. After they are aware it is at your discretion, put them on limited use for a few days. Allow them to earn more time by being responsible.

914. Go to the people they have loaned it to. Make the family and the child aware that you do not allow your child's vehicles to be loaned out, and if it happens again you will consider it theft.

ADD METHODS YOU HAVE USED:

_____
_____
_____
_____

Hanging out the Window

These are for children that are *willing* to cooperate in consequences.

915. Do not allow the child to open the window for the next three rides.
916. Have the child sit in the center seat in the back for the next ride.
917. Give the child choices. They can choose to continue the ride with the window down and sit in their seat, or they can finish the ride with the window up. If they hang out the window again, pull the car over to the side of the road and roll up the window.
918. Once you get home have the child write or say, "I will not hang out the window," ten times. Let them know this is to help them remember to respect your wishes.
919. When you stop, or get ready to ride again, have the child hang out the window for five minutes first. Explain that they need to get all of that out of their system before the car starts to move.

1001 NATURAL LOGICAL CONSEQUENCES

These are for children that are *unwilling* to cooperate in consequences.

920. The next time you are going somewhere, remind the child of their hanging out the window the last time. Do not allow the child in the car until they have said ten times, "I will not hang out the window."
921. Ignore the behavior. The next time the child wants to go somewhere, tell them no, reminding them of their behavior the last time they drove with you. Be sure to let them know you will try it again, the next time they ask.
922. Reward right the behavior. Focus your energy on letting the child know you appreciate what they are doing when they are not hanging out the window.
923. Many windows are such that you can make them unusable. If it is an ongoing pattern with the child, by all means, disable the window for a month and make the child's assigned seat the one next to that window. At the end of the month you can try the child out in other seats to see if the behavior has stopped.
924. Preplan the trip or practice diversion by keeping the child busy doing other things. I find it best to plan in my head what we will be doing in the car, then, go over it with the child.

ADD METHODS YOU HAVE USED:

_____
_____
_____
_____

Hollers out the Window

These are for children that are *willing* to cooperate in consequences.

925. Give the child yelling lessons. Before or after you are going somewhere, have the child yell all the things out of the window they think they might be tempted to yell.
926. If the child has yelled out the window, make them speak in a whisper for the next five minutes. This helps get the decibel level down and destroys the power of being heard by strangers.
927. Do not allow them to get in the car without a plan of action on the next trip. Have them tell you what they are going to do with their time in the car. Stress to the child this is to avoid them yelling out the window.
928. Observe silence for the rest of the trip. Explain that they must need some practice in that, since they haven't yet learned to control their voice level.
929. Make the radio a privilege. Say that you will turn it on only if the child promises not to holler out the window.

1001 NATURAL LOGICAL CONSEQUENCES

These are for children that are *unwilling* to cooperate in consequences.

930. Before the child can get in the car, roll up the window and explain their behavior last time convinced you that the window needs to be up when traveling with them. Stress that if they want the freedom of the window down, they need to show responsibility by leaving it up this trip.
931. Only speak to the child in a whisper for the rest of the ride. Explain to the child since they were yelling out the window you assumed their hearing must be sensitive. So for the rest of the ride you will be speaking softly.
932. Ignore the behavior. Reinforce all the positive behavior during the trip. If there is someone else in the car keep the focus on that person and how they are behaving. Don't say, "Not like_____," no matter how great the temptation.
933. Try to arrange the seating so the child is in the middle of the back seat. If this is impossible, at least have the child sit in the back, explaining that their hollering out of the car is upsetting to you.
934. Make the front seat a privilege. If the child has gone part of the ride without hollering, pull over to the side. Let them know how much you appreciate their behavior and invite them to sit in the front with you. If you currently have a person in the front, let them know you are enjoying them, but you want to reward the behavior from the child.

ADD METHODS YOU HAVE USED:

_____
_____
_____
_____

Addictive Behavior, the Mysterious Maze

I called this the mysterious maze because it lulls you into fighting *symptoms*, rather than the real *cause*. The nature of addiction itself has so many ramifications, so many areas of life it touches, that it seems impossible to get to the basic problem.

In my color chart I colored it brown, because it is without its own distinction and seems to blend into all other behaviors. It is probably the hardest to fight because you shadow box all the time with it. I will be the first to say that I have never successfully consequated an addiction with the result of the addiction stopping. The only result I have ever achieved is an awareness in the child and the child's willingness to look at it for what it is.

The best answer I can offer for parent's, is for them to go to Alanon, or some other support group that helps them to deal with the nature of addiction as it pertains to you. I have found these people to have a realm of experience that is not only useful, but *vital* in dealing with these types of problems. The nature of addiction is a medical one and although many might disagree, the AMA has classified it as a disease and if your child is showing many of the symptoms and signs of addiction, you would be wise to seek medical help. If the behaviors are such that you are unsure whether it is a true addiction, or simply experimentation, these consequences will help you to see it in a clearer light.

Tips to remember:
1. Addiction is subtle, getting you to focus on symptoms rather than the real problem.
2. It is colored brown because it blends in subtly with other behaviors.
3. The best help for *you* is an Alanon group.
4. The most probable outcome is increased awareness in you and the child.
5. Addiction is a **disease** and needs to be treated as such.

Compulsive Cleaning or Movement

After letting you know AA and Alanon meetings are the answer, it seems strange that I am starting with a behavior there is no fellowship for. I have seen some children who show these signs for compulsive obsessive behavior. They may need *medication* and the child will often show remarkable results once they are on it. You may need to **consult a psychiatrist**.

These are for children that are *willing* to cooperate in consequences.

935. Set in as much structure as possible. Have the child plan their day including time frames. Allow them to check off each thing as it is done.
936. Set in a quiet or recreational time each day. Use video games or some other thing that gives the feeling of activity without much movement; stress that you approve of their inactivity.
937. Set in a time period for some slow structured activity. Have the child practice ballet or karate; making the movements slow and deliberate.
938. Have the child retrace their footsteps sharing with you the mistakes that are made by over doing. Allow them to see this is not a help.
939. Buy the child a rocking chair or a rocking horse. Set in a time each day for sitting in it. This again will satisfy the urge for movement in a settling way.

These are for children that are *unwilling* to cooperate in consequences.

940. Allow the privilege of helping only as long as the child is willing to slow down. You will need to make it clear to the child that you cannot risk broken things or bad feelings that occur when the child is in constant motion.
941. Structure the child's time into small compartments such as the car, or their room. Do **not** make it appear that you are punishing them. Simply plan activities that will somewhat confine their actions. Help them to appreciate inactivity.
942. Ignore the behavior. Give it no praise or attention. Often this type of a child will move from there into a martyrdom mode. Gently let them know the type of cleaning they are doing is not a help. Praise all activities that are calm.
943. Plan their day with a rest or reading time. **Do not** make it mandatory, but do offer some small reward if they are willing to participate.
944. Bring the child to the Doctor and have the Doctor assess the behavior and make sure nothing is medically wrong.

ADD METHODS YOU HAVE USED:

_____
_____
_____
_____

Drinking Alcohol

For all young people, experimental behavior is likely to occur. The consequences set below will be extremely effective for them. The continuation of drinking or setting the priority to drink *above all else* is the sign of an addictive type personality. Addiction is a *disease* and will need treatment.

These are for children that are *willing* to cooperate in consequences.

945. Make the child aware of the consequences. Have them do a report on the physical affects of drinking on the brain and the body.
946. Withdraw all unsupervised going out, for a week. Allow the child to earn that back by showing responsible behavior such as telling you who they got the liquor from.
947. Have the child call the police and tell them they were a minor and drinking. Make sure they find out the penalty to the adult who sold them the liquor.
948. Have them go back to where they got the liquor and tell the person they are under age and they are sorry that they almost got them in trouble. If it is a person who is aware of their age, have them go with you, to tell the person they are no longer allowed to hang out with them.
949. Have them go to five A.A. speaker meetings. This will do *much* toward educating them on alcoholism. Make sure that they are meetings that are open to the public before you bring them.

These are for children that are *unwilling* to cooperate in consequences.

950. Allow the child the natural consequences of the behavior; a hangover, vomiting, and less money. When the child complains, good naturally say something like, "If you want to play, you have got to pay." Do nothing to ease the child's discomfort (also known as **enabling**).

951. Hold a **family meeting** and as a group share your experience and some literature on the dangers of drinking. Make the child aware if it continues, you will **look into a treatment program**.

952. Make a dedicated effort to find out where the child got the liquor. Start calling the friends that they were with and tracking down all clues. If you find the person, tell them if it happens again, or you see them with your child, you plan on prosecuting.

953. Remove all privileges to earn money for a while, explaining that you no longer trust the child's ability to use it wisely. A second choice on this would be for you to hold all money that the child earns for a short period of time.

ADD METHODS YOU HAVE USED:

_____
_____
_____
_____
_____

Smoking Cigarettes

I must again say that a certain amount of teen experimentation is normal and these consequences will work on this type of behavior.

These are for children that are *willing* to cooperate in consequences.

954. Confront the child in a **family meeting**. Discuss the fact that smoking is illegal for them and that the whole family could be hurt due to the fire hazard. Let the other family members share their experiences with smoking.
955. Require the child to do a three page report on the hazards of smoking. I insist on at least two references.
956. Allow the child the choice, but be explicit in that you will not permit it in your home and you will not contribute by buying them. Have the child do a thorough report on the information about smoking before they decide.
957. Take the child to a cancer section of your local hospital or allow them to talk to someone who has lung cancer. Be sure to make them aware that knowing they are smoking, you want them armed with all the information.

These are for children that are *unwilling* to cooperate in consequences.

958. Call the parents of your child's friends. Let them know that you have caught your child smoking. Ask if they would be interested in helping make the local children aware. Check your resources to see if you can get a nurse or doctor to speak to the children.

959. Confiscate all allowances and earned money. Instead, let the child earn credits that you will spend on what they want.

960. Take the child to the doctor and make the doctor aware that the child is smoking. Have the doctor talk to the child about the harmful effects.

961. Do not confront the behavior. Instead, plan a time when you and the child can go see a friend or acquaintance who is an ex-smoker. Once there, let the child know you are aware that they have been smoking. Explain that the friend used to smoke and would be glad to share how and why they stopped.

ADD METHODS YOU HAVE USED:
_____
_____
_____
_____

Using Drugs

Although this behavior is quite similar to drinking in its answers, because the legal problems are at higher risk, and the availability always from an "illegal source", the action is somewhat stronger.

These are for children that are *willing* to cooperate in consequences.

962. Confront the behavior immediately. Get the names of the other people who were involved and call all parents making them aware of the problem. Make all contacts with these people supervised for at least a month.
963. Have the child go to a treatment center and talk to addicts who are striving for recovery. They will share some of what got them there. Once you bring the child home, have them write a list of the losses that could have occurred just from casual using.
964. Make all availability to money off limits for a month. If they work, have them turn the paycheck over to you and you buy what they need for a month.
965. Have the child volunteer some time at a local hospital or treatment center. Explain that this will allow them to see first hand some of the dangers that lie ahead.
966. Have them go to at least three Narcotic's Anonymous meetings. Tell the child that although you don't yet believe they are an addict you want them to be aware that if they cannot stop there are places available to them.

These are for children that are *unwilling* to cooperate in consequences.

967. Call in the police. Have them get the names of the other people involved. Also, ask them what will be involved for your child. As a parent with first hand experience, I know how hard this is, but I had to realize I was dealing with a potentially life threatening substance.
968. Start spot (room checks). Let the child know that trust has been broken and you must feel secure that they are no longer abusing the privilege of their privacy.
969. Call teachers and the parents of the child's friend's. Make the community aware of your concerns and ask for help in monitoring the child's actions.
970. Call your minister or a local Narcotic's Anonymous hot line and ask if they have a person who would be willing to come out and talk to your child about the dangers of drug use.
971. If the problem is ongoing, do not overlook having the child placed in a drug rehabilitation treatment center. The ongoing use is a strong indicator of an addicted person and if that's what you are dealing with it is bound to get worse.

ADD METHODS YOU HAVE USED:

_____
_____
_____
_____

Compulsive Eating

Many times children like us, eat to cover other things they are feeling. Most of these consequences are designed to get at the feelings. But if this is a longstanding problem or ongoing you might wish to seek professional help. There is the *risk in teenagers of* **anorexia** *or* **bulimia**.

These are for children that are *willing* to cooperate in consequences.

972. Make all food with permission only. If the child asks, rather than say "No" ask, "Why are you wanting that?" Help the child sort through to a reason. Then allow the child the choice.
973. Have the child do something active such as taking a walk before they can have the desired food. This will act as a diversion and raise the energy level, decreasing hunger.
974. Help the child with an eating plan. Get a calorie book, plan menus and snacks, do not bring food into the house that you know the child is extremely fond of for several weeks. Give lots of support when the child goes by the plan.
975. Create a chart with an eating plan. In it, put things to do that will burn the calories that the child is about to eat. An example would be a candy bar = six miles running. Then have the child choose the food plus the activity included. Note: this will only work with a willing child, to use it on an unwilling child is a setup for lying.
976. Make the child sit and share one concern they are having with you before they eat what they want. After they share it, ask them if they are sure that it wouldn't be easier to solve the problem than to "eat" at it.

These are for children that are *unwilling* to cooperate in consequences.

977. Allow the child to continue the eating, but start writing down all they consume. Wait for a pleasant moment, then confront the problem and try to get the child to see the likely consequences and become cooperative in a plan of action.
978. Ignore the behavior, but remain confrontive. When the child complains of things they can not do, or clothes that don't fit, say, non-judgmentally, that they have a choice as to how they eat and the results.
979. Make the child responsible for the cost of all food above the normal amount. Use a calorie counter or a doctor to confirm this. When you do your weekly shopping, calculate the child's costs. This will help the child with their awareness.
980. Bring the child to the doctor and have the doctor address the health issues. Sit with the doctor and come up with a plan for other choices the child can make besides eating.
981. Manipulate the environment. Plan in activities that will keep the child busy and away from food. This will also build in habits of handling things in a different manner than eating.

ADD METHODS YOU HAVE USED:
_____
_____
_____
_____

Bigotry, Born Better People

This is a state of mind which is probably more destructive to the people engaged in it than any of us realize. I colored it black and it shades every other color into a darker shade. Whether the self righteous person, or the angry person, when you add the black of prejudice you get worse behavior. I would like to take just a moment and look at the faces of prejudice. I think we are all pretty inclined to see it as color related, but this is a lie. If I am a Christian and have no tolerance for an atheist I am prejudiced. If I hang with a group of bikers and hate the yuppies I am prejudiced. If I only accept those into my world from the golf club set, I am prejudiced. Any time I judge another by a group I am engaging in prejudice. Do I gripe at the tourists driving? It is prejudice. Whether we choose to like it or lump it, if it is invading our home and present in our children, we had best make sure we are not teaching it.

I think all of us like to feel somewhat "better" than those we do not admire, but do we have the right to? I do believe we all make judgments on people, and if you have read this far I am sure you realize that I feel there are certain groups we are better off not around. But that is the group, *not* the individual. I think each person must be taken on their own merit and we must all be responsible for our own actions. I also believe that different people in our lives add spice and make for flavorful living.

To know I set my own limits is what truly makes the difference; overcoming the natural desire for all of us to live in the *safe* zone; that place where we know how people act and react. We should learn to take healthy risks and set good boundaries. We ought to know what we will and won't accept. This is half of the trick to overcoming prejudice. The other half is in looking at the individual rather than the group. When I catch myself saying "them" I realize I am blocking my own self growth and teaching my kids to do the same. It matters little if my prejudice is the people of a different religion who teach the God of hell and damnation, instead of my God of love, or my child's intolerance of the race of children at school, it is the same. They are learning how to group people who are different from us. The skills are learned and sadly they are almost always learned at home. I have discovered this from bitter experience. I could not understand the amount of prejudice in my home, for I considered myself a relatively unprejudiced person. This was not true. I simply was not a particularly *racially* prejudiced person. So examine yourself, if you see this monster, stomp it out; not only in your kids, but in yourself. Whether you realize it or not it will block friends, housing, job opportunities, and almost every other endeavor of a meaningful life experience.

Tips to remember:
1. I color it black because it darkens all other behaviors.
2. It has many faces, it is not just racial.
3. It usually is learned in the home.
4. It gives the feeling one is better than a group.
5. It takes away our choices.
6. It can be outgrown by not grouping people and by having clear boundaries

Name Calling

These are for children that are *willing* to cooperate in consequences.

982. Have the child give a definition of the word and why they think it relates to that individual.
983. Have the child come up with three to five ways they could have addressed the person that might have been less hurtful.
984. Have them write a letter of apology to the person. Explaining what they plan to do in the future.
985. If it is a stranger, have the child meet a person of the same group and spend at least an hour in your home or a public place with them, then ask them how they would feel calling that name to the person they were just with.

These are for children that are *unwilling* to cooperate in consequences.

986. Set in an awareness week. For that week, or couple of days, all the people in the house are to discover and mimic one or more things about the group. Offer a prize to the one who does the best. Include food, talk, dress, heritage, and customs.
987. Make the child watch a film that will make them more aware before they can watch any other movies. Supervise this, since they may choose a film that will only further their own beliefs.
988. Make a friend of the group that you see the prejudice in. Have the person around. Allow the child to get to know them. Choose your time and then connect the child's behavior with the reality of the person.
989. Share five to seven names you have been called and how they made you feel. Ask the child to share some names they may have been called and how they felt, but do not insist.

ADD METHODS YOU HAVE USED:

_____
_____
_____
_____

Joining Questionable Groups

I wish to make it clear that I am speaking of groups that foster the put down of any other group of people; a supremacy type theory, whether that be an outlaw gang or the Klu Klux Klan.

These are for children that are *willing* to cooperate in consequences.

990. Just say no. I am a big believer that this is a choice you can make, but not while that choice influences everyone in the house. It delays the process.
991. Have the child explore the background of the group. What its actions have been and what the results of the members have been. Allow them to be sure that they can live with the results of joining. If the child is still determined, allow them two friends from the group, but in your home and supervised.
992. Give the child alternatives. List the activities around and give them a choice of any of the ones that they would like to be a part of. Explain that the choice of that group is not an option.
993. Give them a cause. Sit and listen to the reasons why they wish to be part of this group. Try to understand what the child's needs are. Offer a more acceptable plan of action. Delay the decision of whether or not they can continue until after the need has been met another way. For example, Jane is all set to become part of the Jets a white antagonist group. In talking, it seems to her that whites get all the privileges. Put her in touch with an equal rights law expert. Have her work through the legal system and then discuss whether she still wants to join the Jets.

These are for children that are *unwilling* to cooperate in consequences.

994. Go to the authorities. Make them aware this is a group that you would prefer your child not be part of. Ask them to come and let your child know that you have informed them of this and that if your child is seen with these people your child will be brought home.
995. Manipulate the time the child has. If their time is filled up, there is no time left to get into a group. Simply keep planning activities. Most of the time it is a peer pressure situation so avoidance will work.
996. Try to gain an ally. Go to the school counselor, or another professional person. Have them spend time with the child. Confront the problem with them and have them address it with the child.
997. Utilize the church and your child's spiritual beliefs. Look up all you can find about the values of the group and the values of your child. Point out the differences. Have a minister or youth pastor talk to the child. Try to get the child interested in changing things with a more appropriate group.

ADD METHODS YOU HAVE USED:

_____
_____
_____
_____

Catch Them Being Good

If this book were to have a most important page this would be it. This is the behavior that lightens the color of all the others. If you were to trash every consequence in this book and simply use this you would be happy with the results.

Too often we lose sight of the fact that not too long ago there was a little boy driving his mom crazy, he would grow up and be president. Two little boys, who, years down the road were to invent the computer, once had a worried mom or dad. A little girl who had the same problems as yours grew up to be a movie star. You see, the mystery of this is when you are dealing with little people, you just don't know the greatness you could be handling. Today an actress, a writer, a politician, an inventor, a great spiritual leader, they were born, they were raised. You could be the mom or dad doing it. Find that talent, see the greatness in your child, it is there, and the child will see it clearer if you see it first and encourage it.

Did they get up and face the day today? Did they clean their room, kiss you, or say I'm sorry? These are all good things that build on creative greatness. Did they take pride in their appearance, write a story, or color a picture? These are the small good things to catch them doing. Did they take a stand, go to church, or offer a prayer? Then they are starting to develop a moral fiber and that is good. Did they make a friend; keep a friend, reason out a problem? These are the skills of social betterment. No, it is not on a grand level yet and it may even be full of wrong judgments, but trust me, no one starts great, but everyone starts.

Today and every day **catch your child being good**. See the small things that they do. Let them know how very special they are and who knows, they might believe you and become something unbelievable.

To each parent who reads this goes my heartfelt prayers and empathy. Your job is challenging but rewarding. My hope is that this book helps, and with all the errors that we are sure to make, that you discover the wonder of that little person living right there, with you.

These are for children that are *willing* to cooperate in consequences.
998. A word of admiration.
999. A hug and a kiss.
1000. A game of cards.
1001. A day sharing the adventure of living.
1002. A hot fudge sundae with two spoons.

These are for children that are *unwilling* to cooperate in consequences.
1003. Do their chore for them.
1004. A note of appreciation over the loud speaker at school or church.
1005. A surprise party for no reason.
1006. A note or a card left by their pillow.
1007. Brag in front of them to your friends.

ADD METHODS YOU HAVE USED:

_____
_____
_____
_____

ADD METHODS YOU HAVE USED: